Billy-Piggy

chapter 10

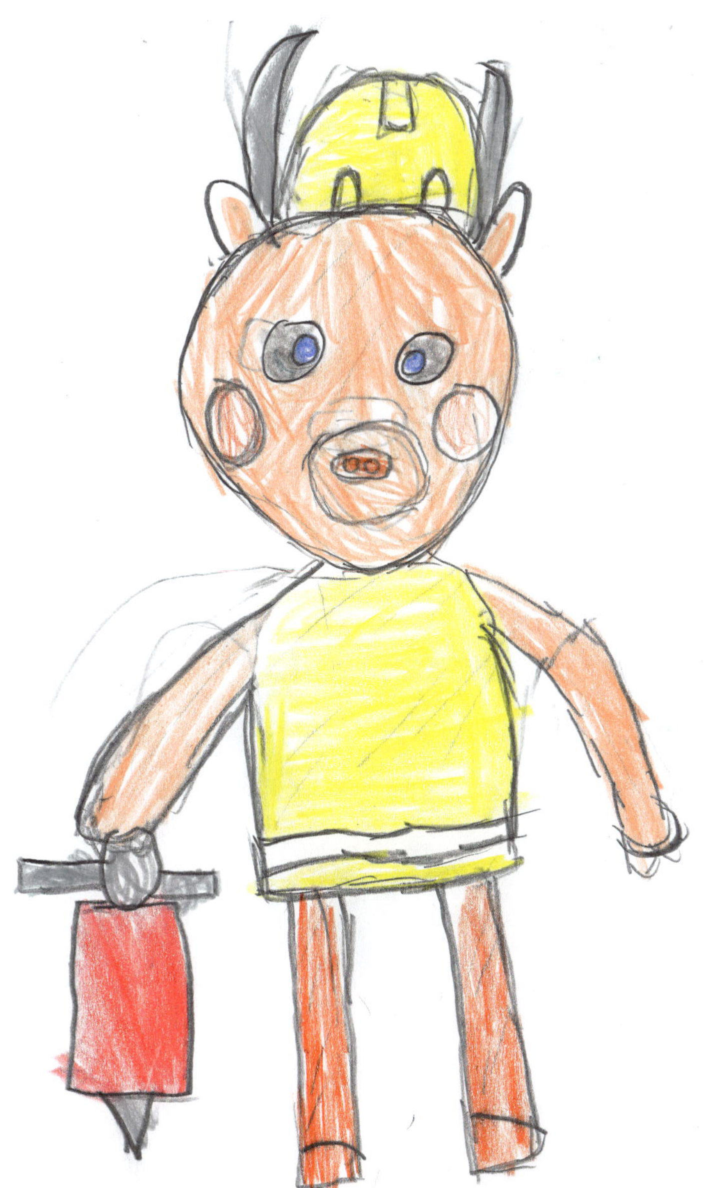

AKUL SAGARE

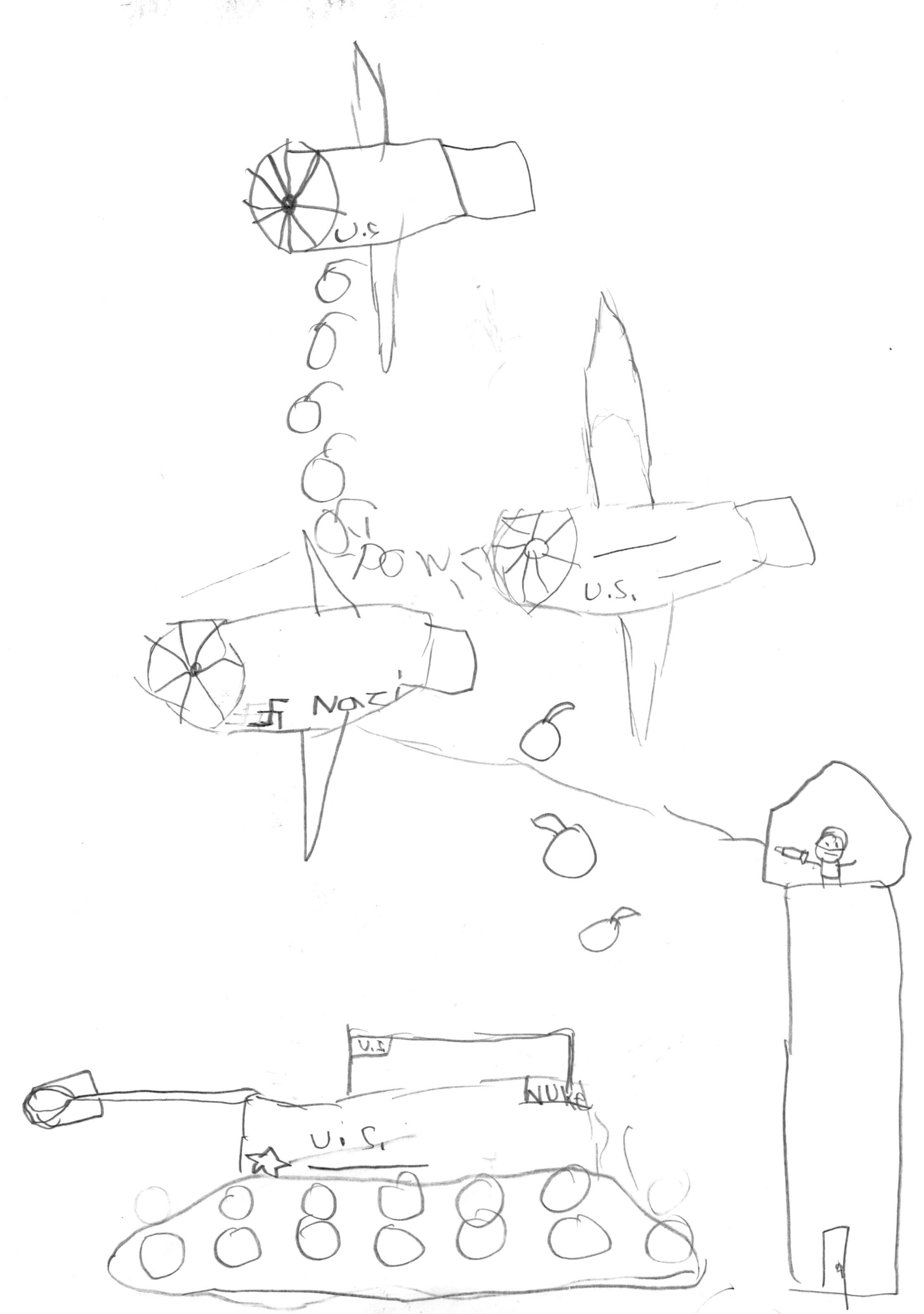
U.S
POW
U.S.
Nazi
U.S
Nuke
U.S

Doggy

piggy chater
4 forset

Akul Sagar

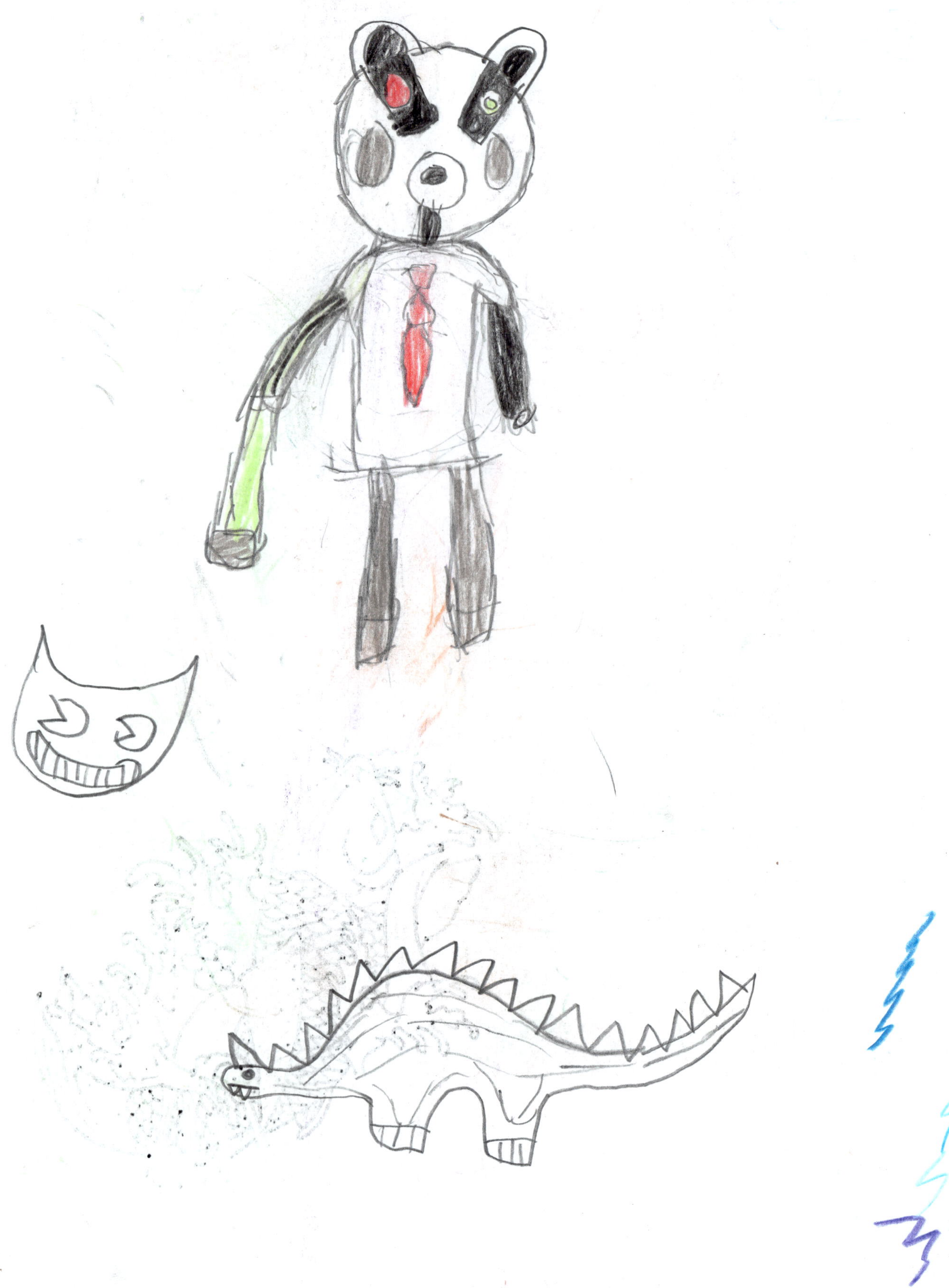

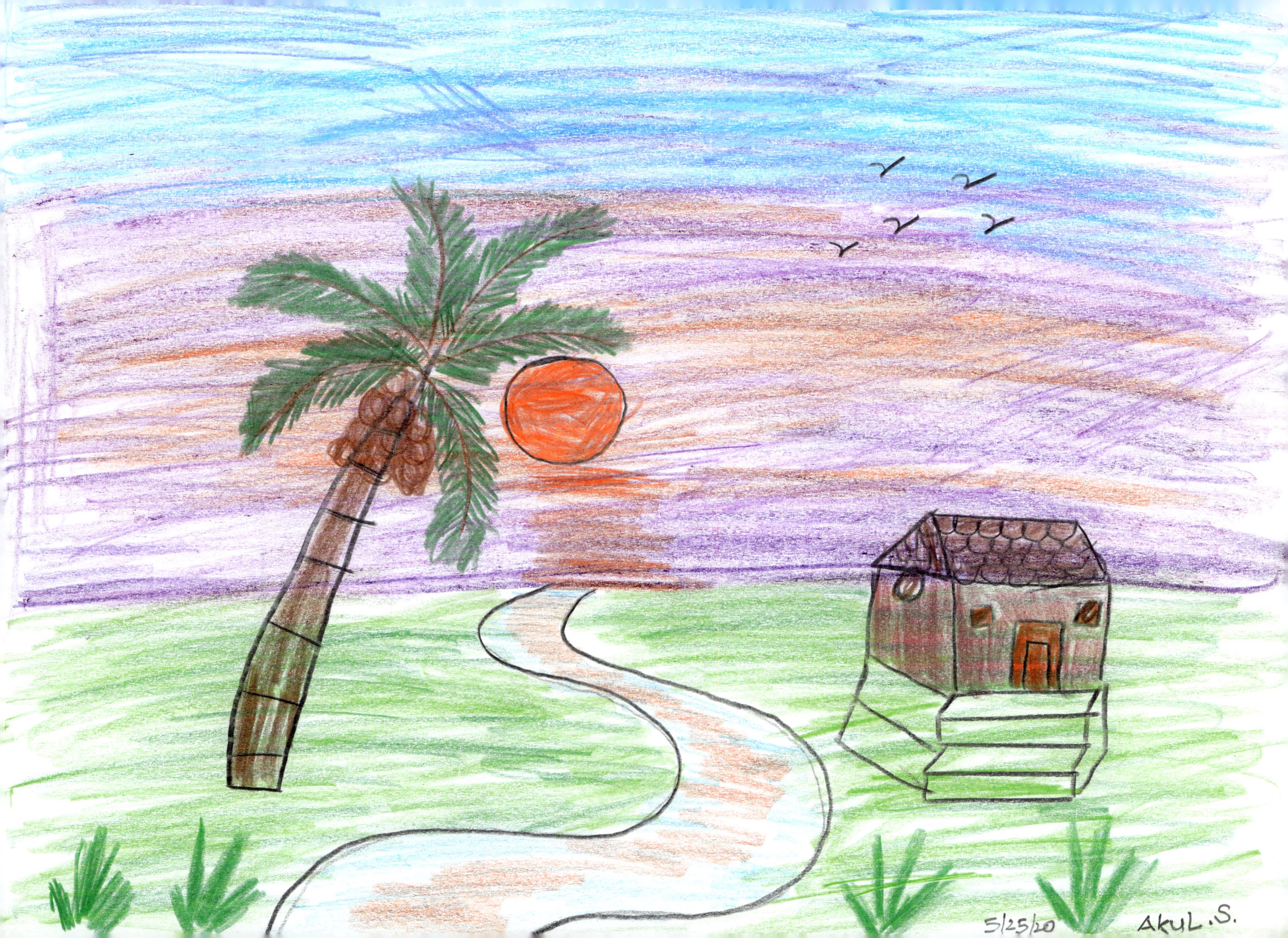
5/25/20
AkuL.S.

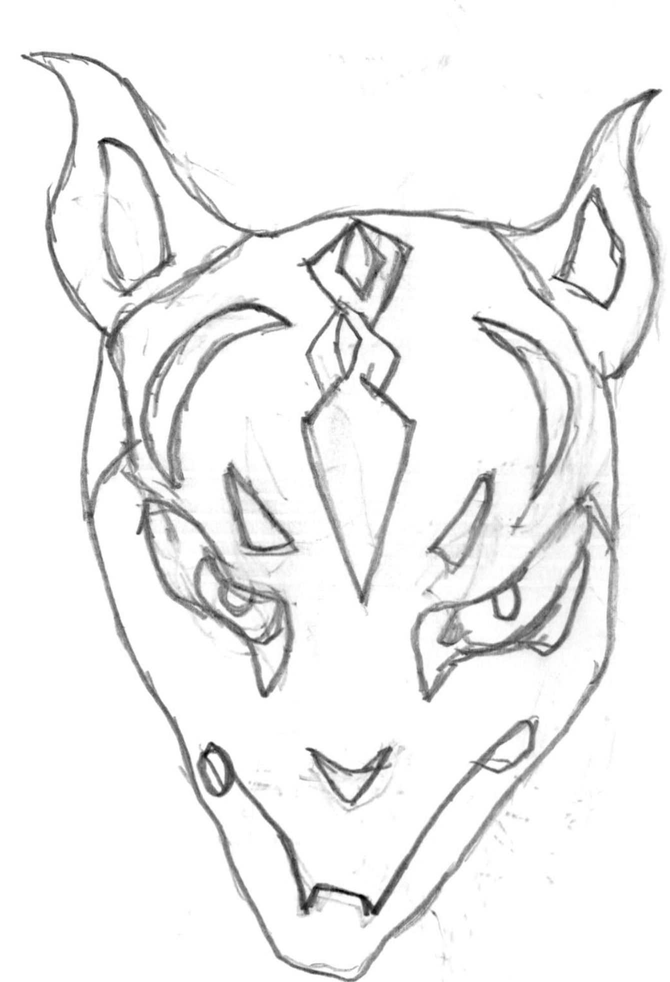

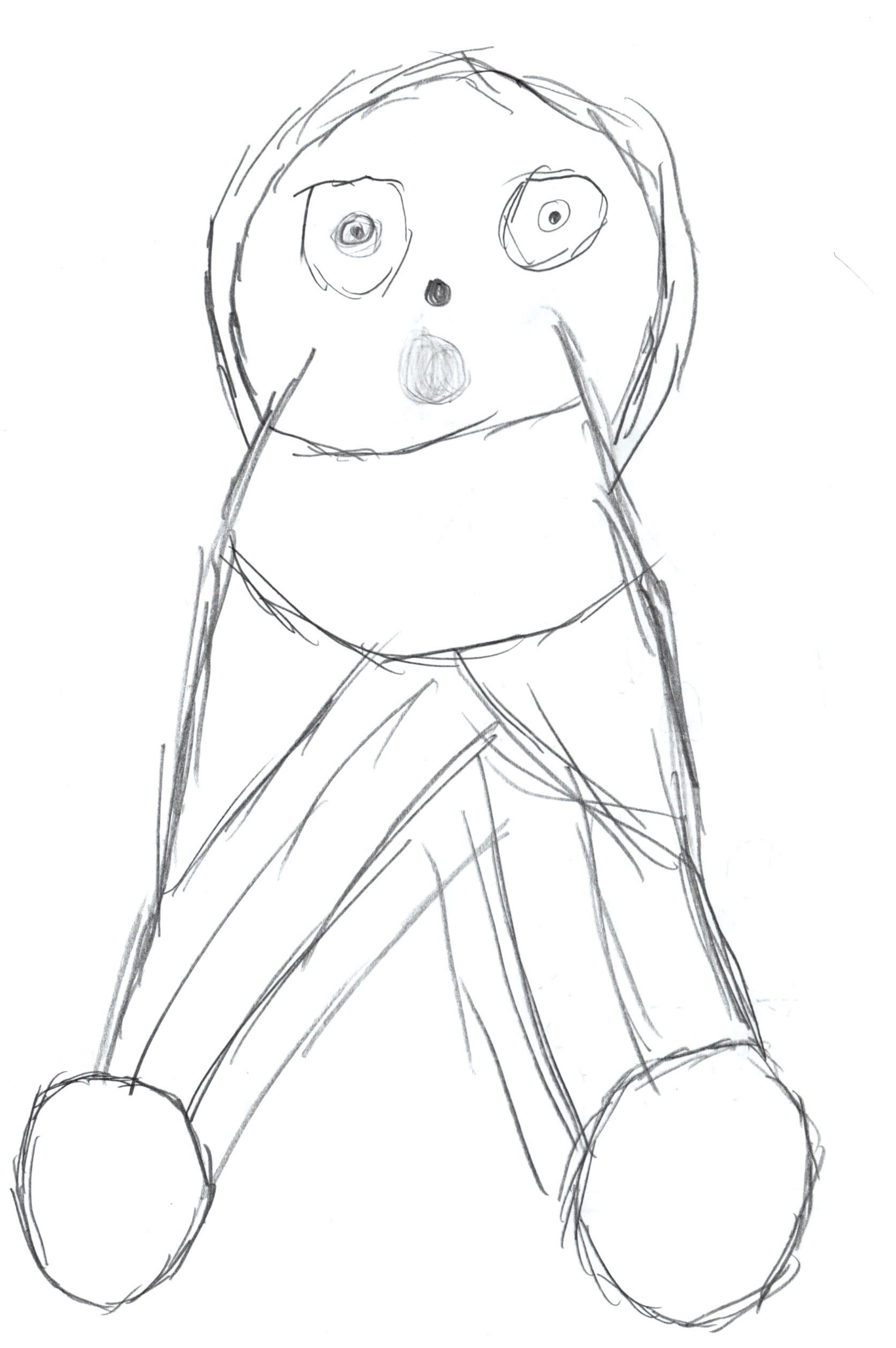

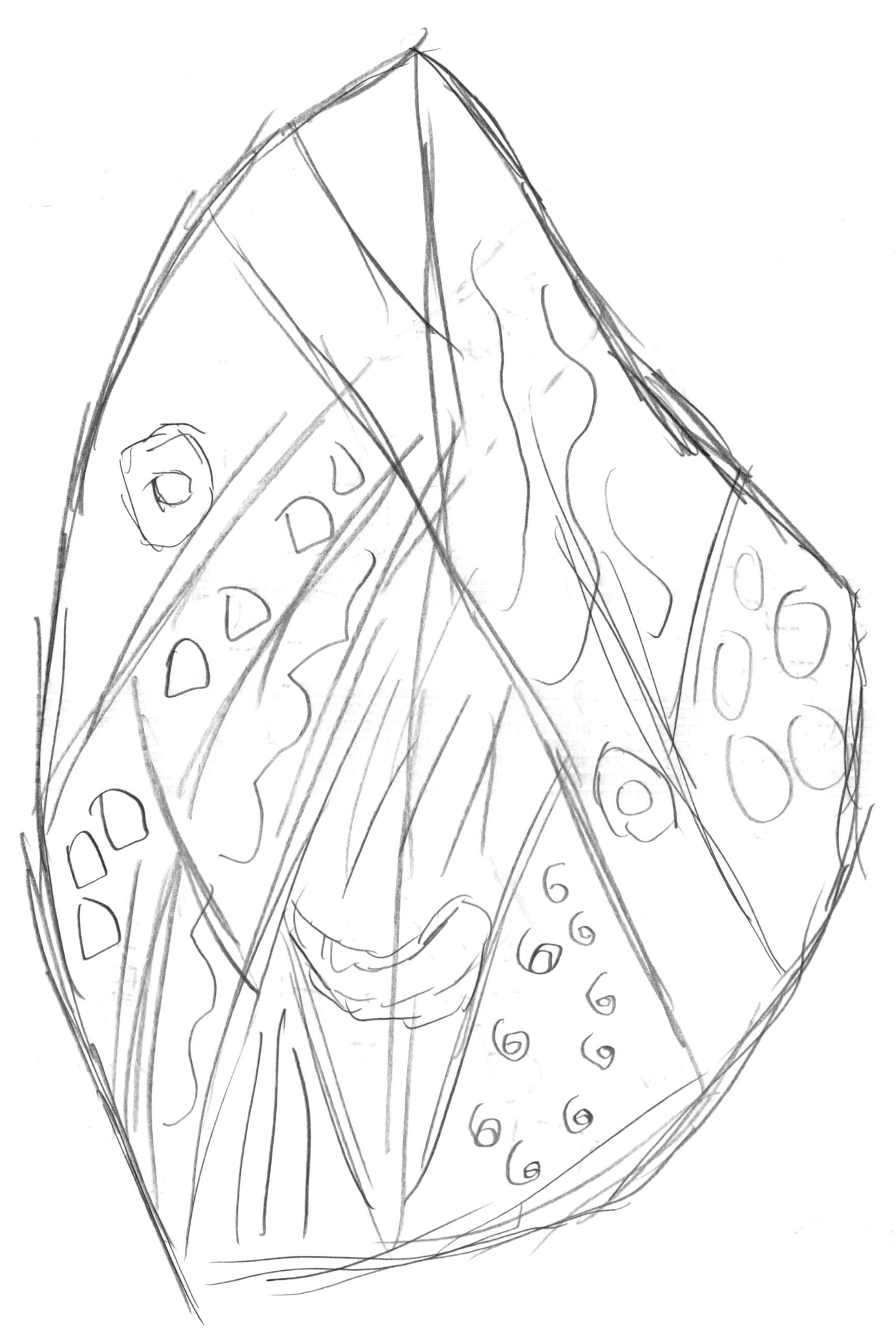

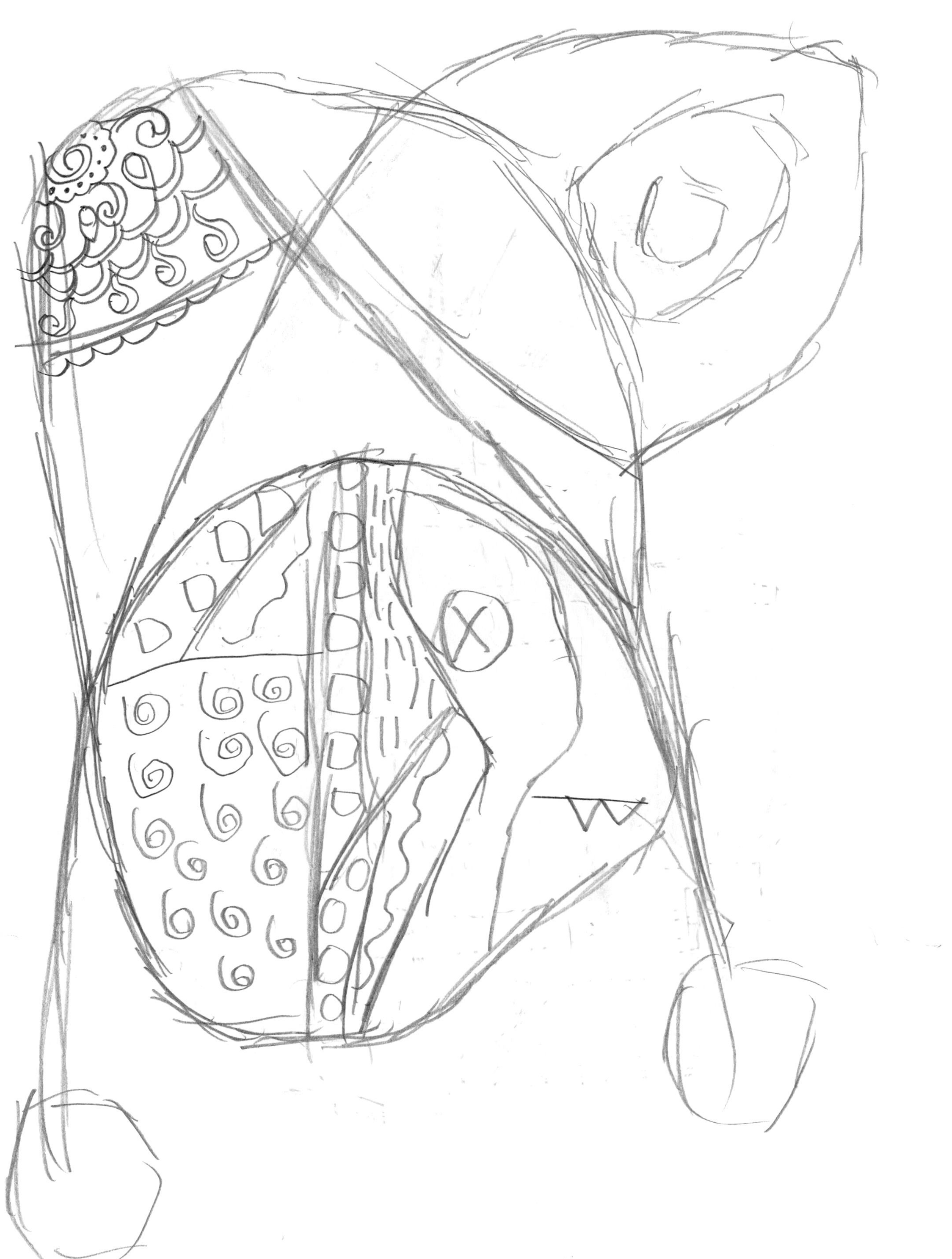

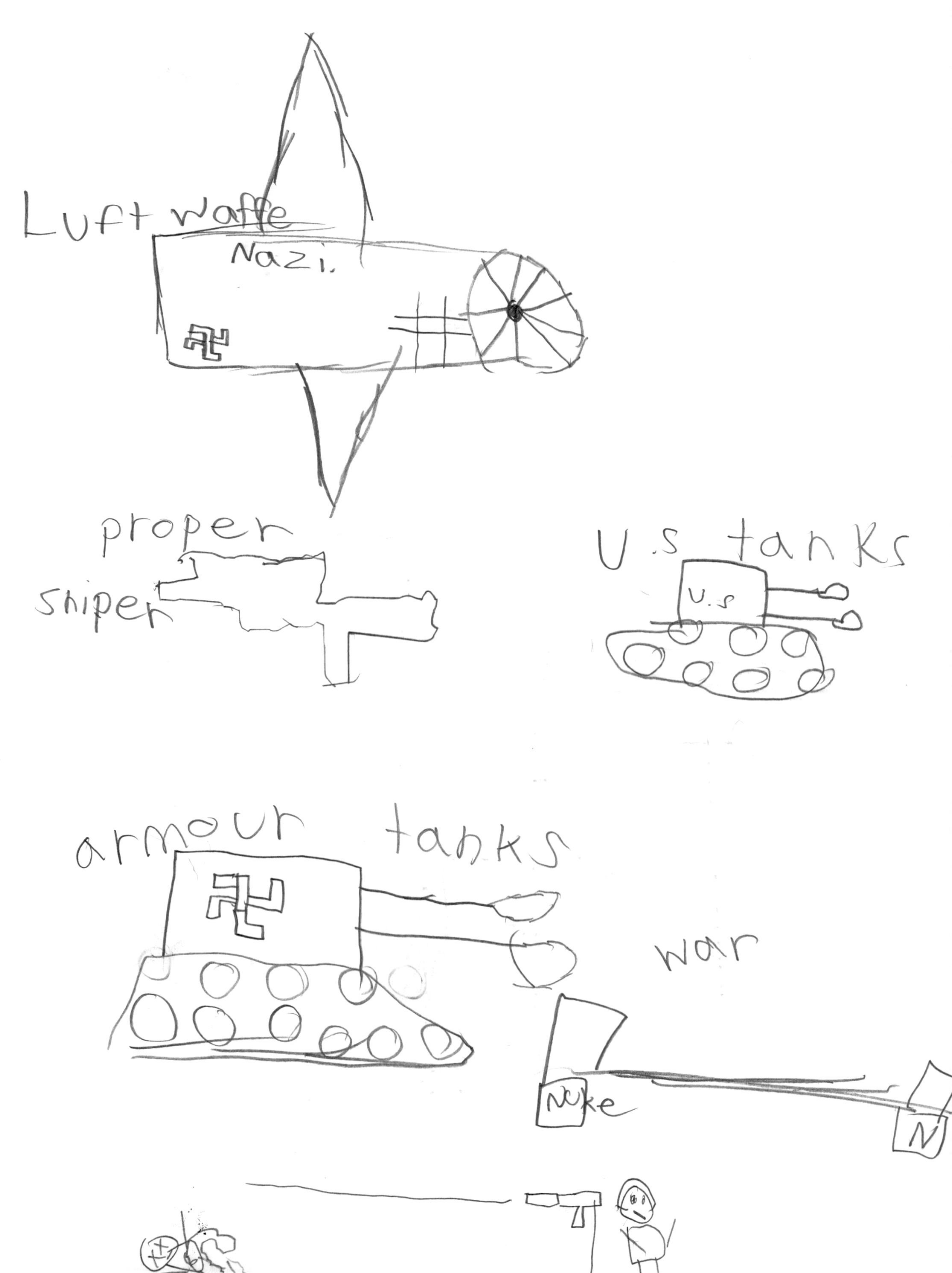
Luftwaffe
Nazi.
proper
sniper
U.S tanks
U.S
armour tanks
war
Nuke
N

Warship

U.S. B. titanic

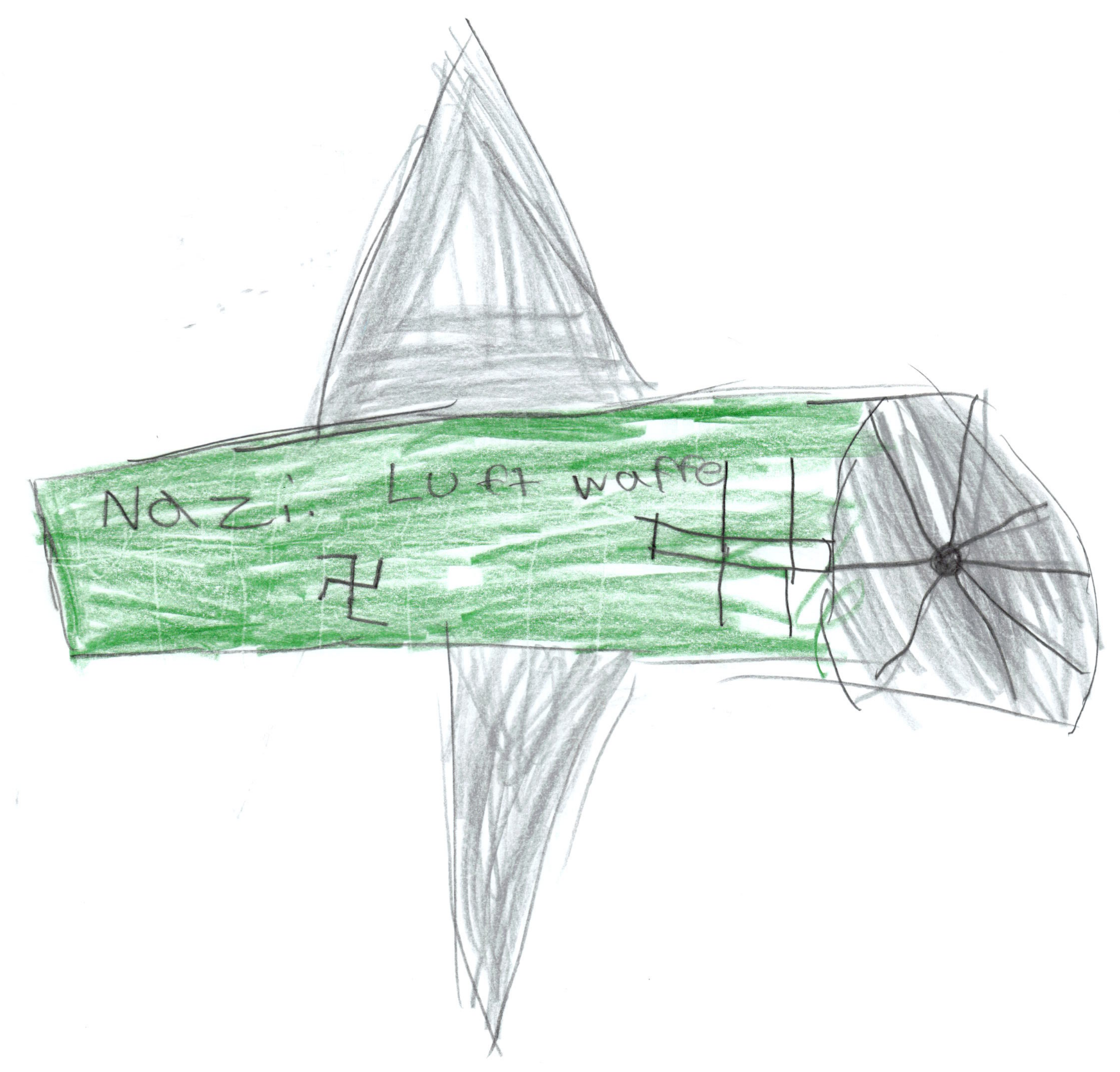
Nazi. Luft waffe

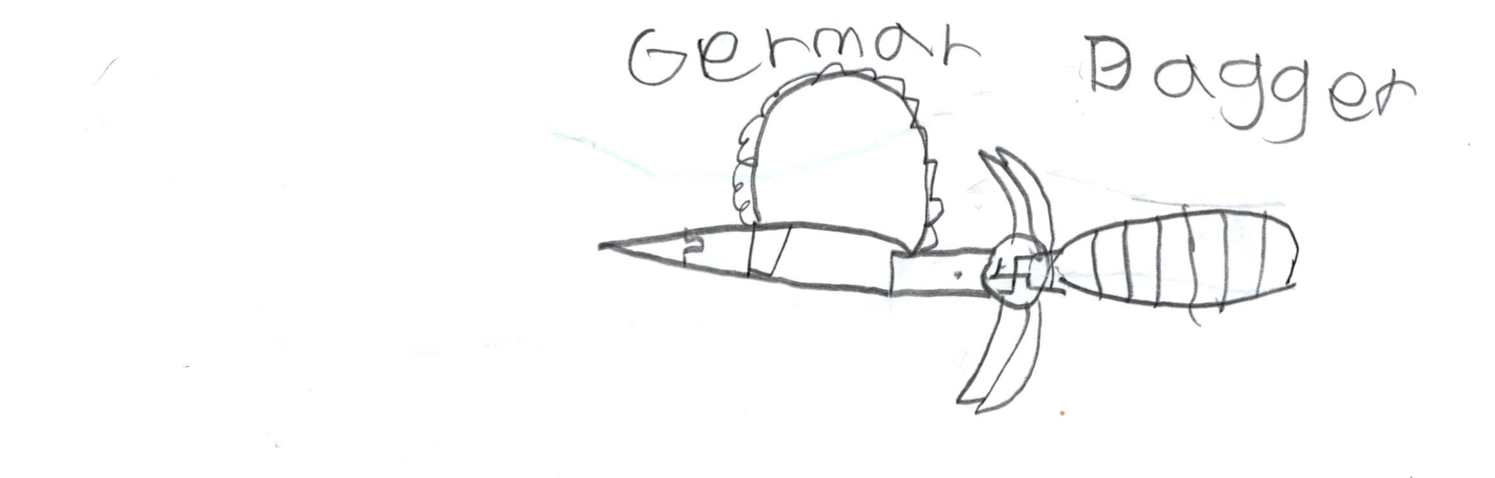
German Dagger

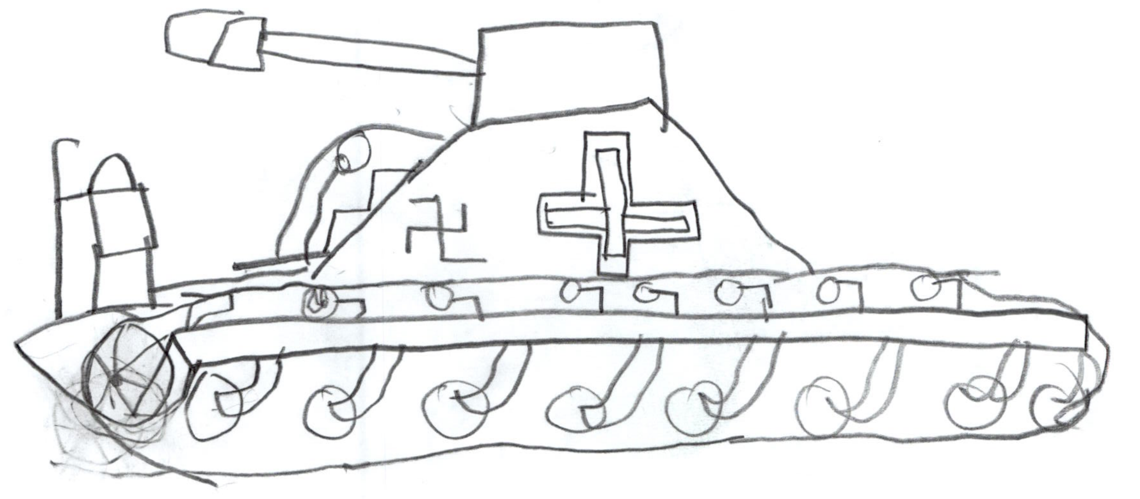

cute cat
ispired by
pusheen

BY AKUl

sea monster

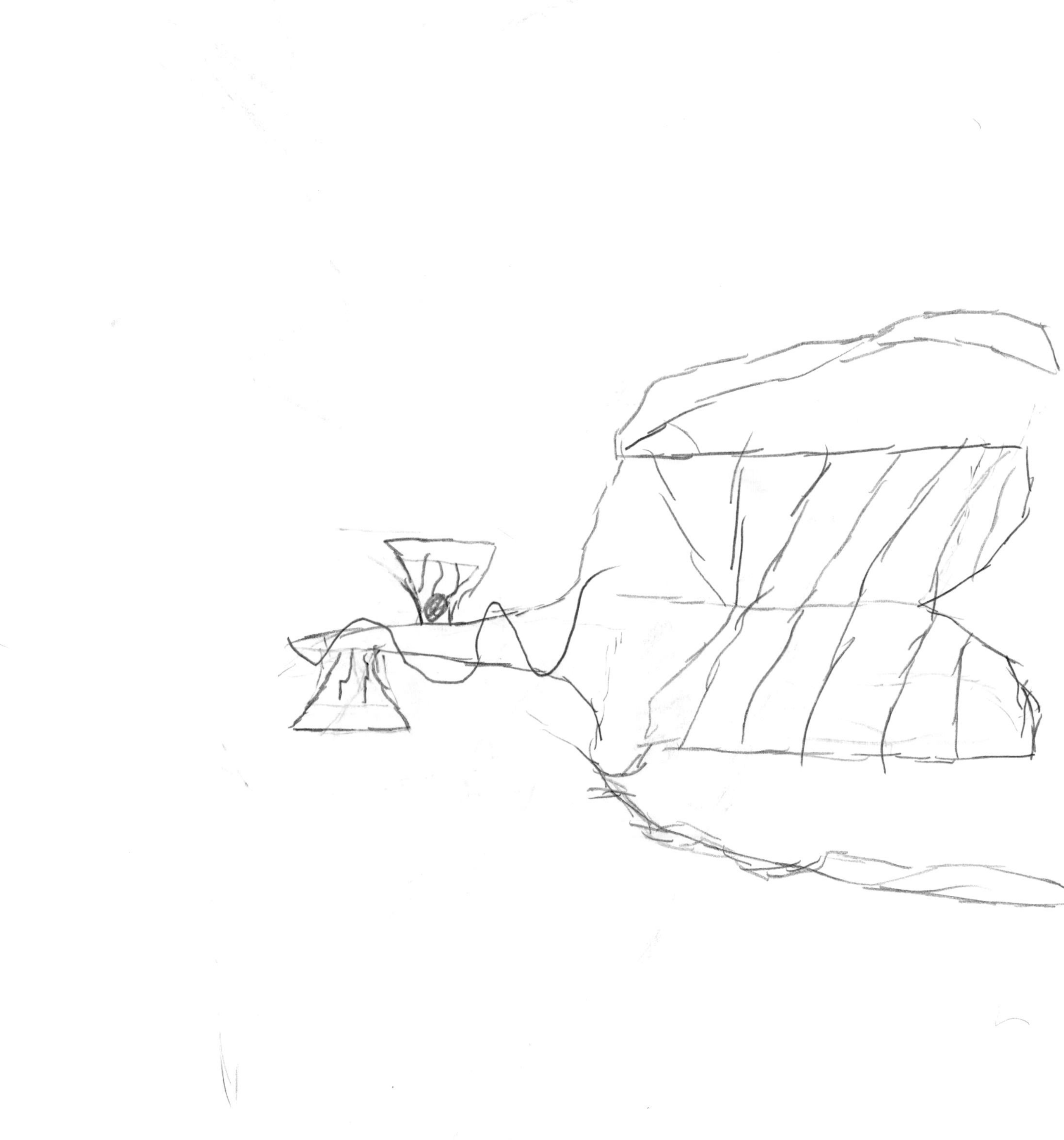

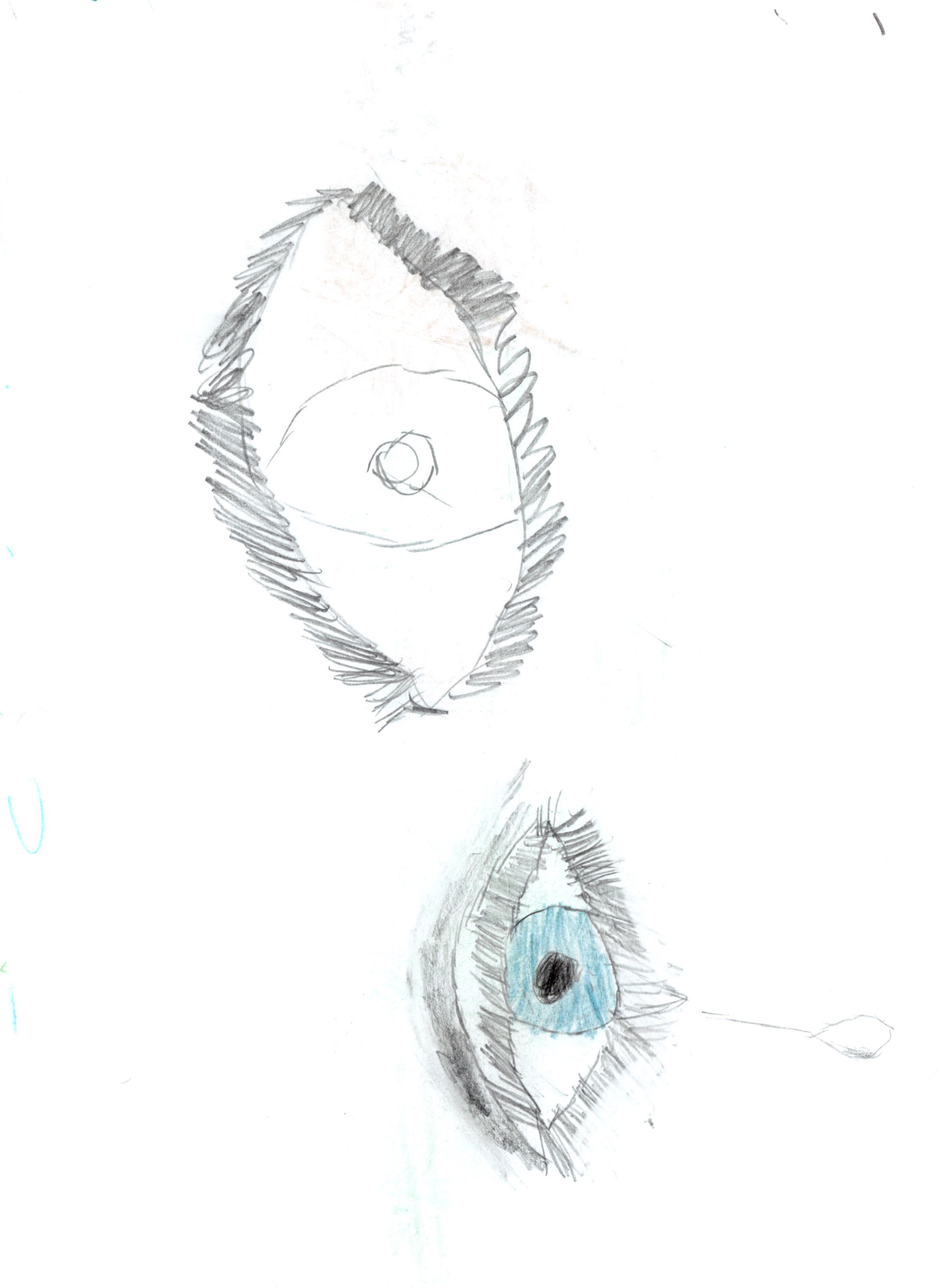

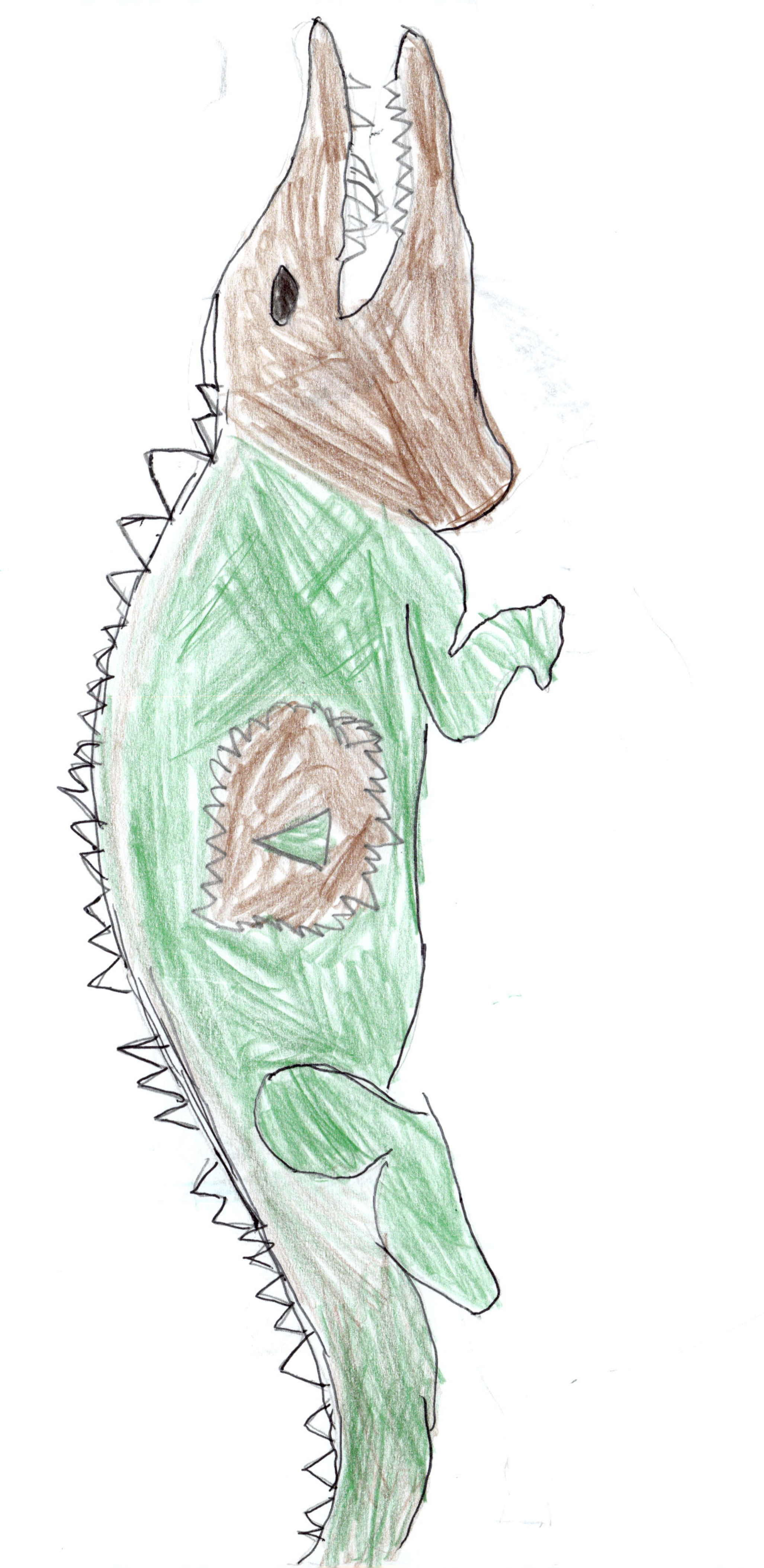

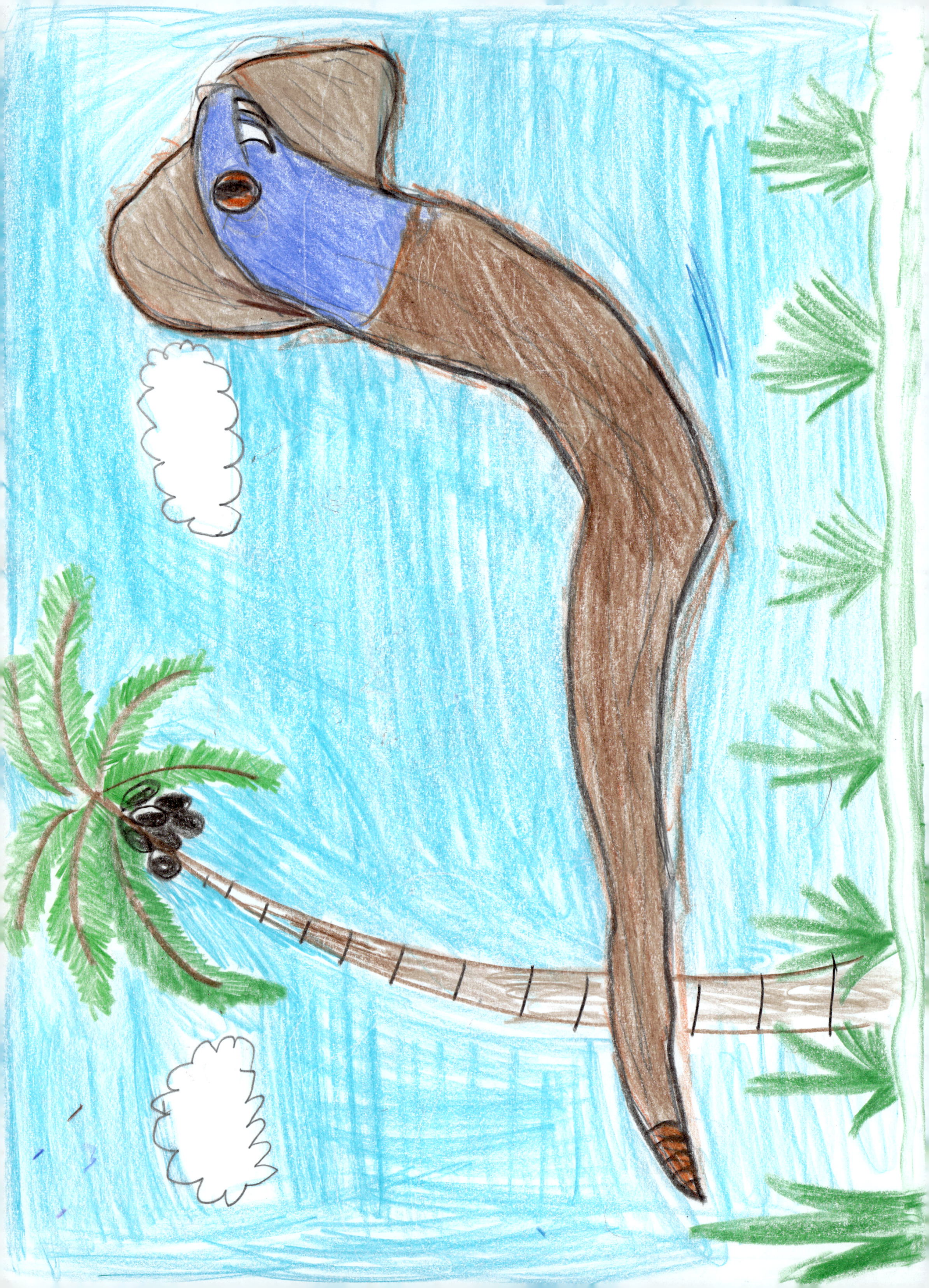

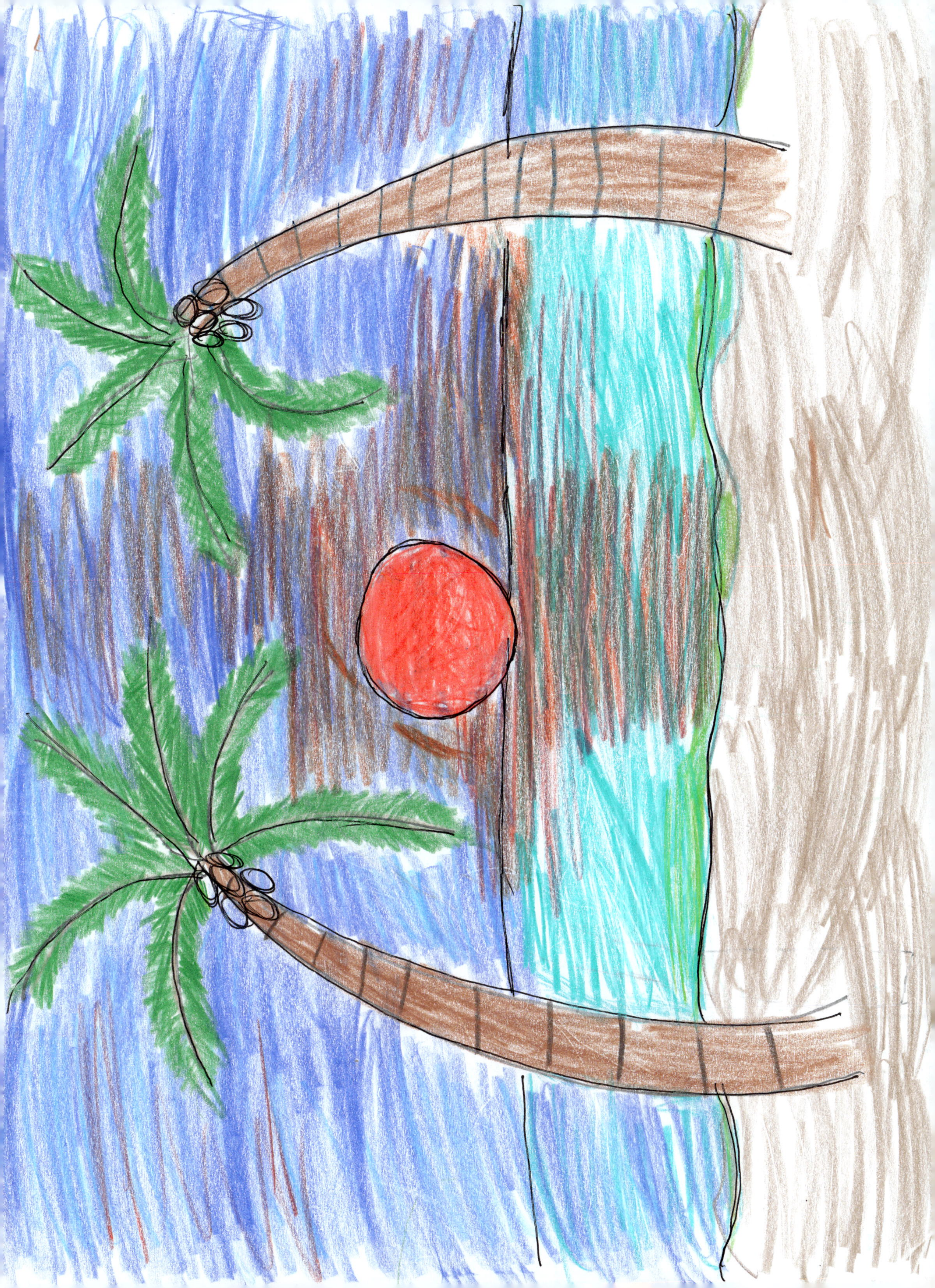

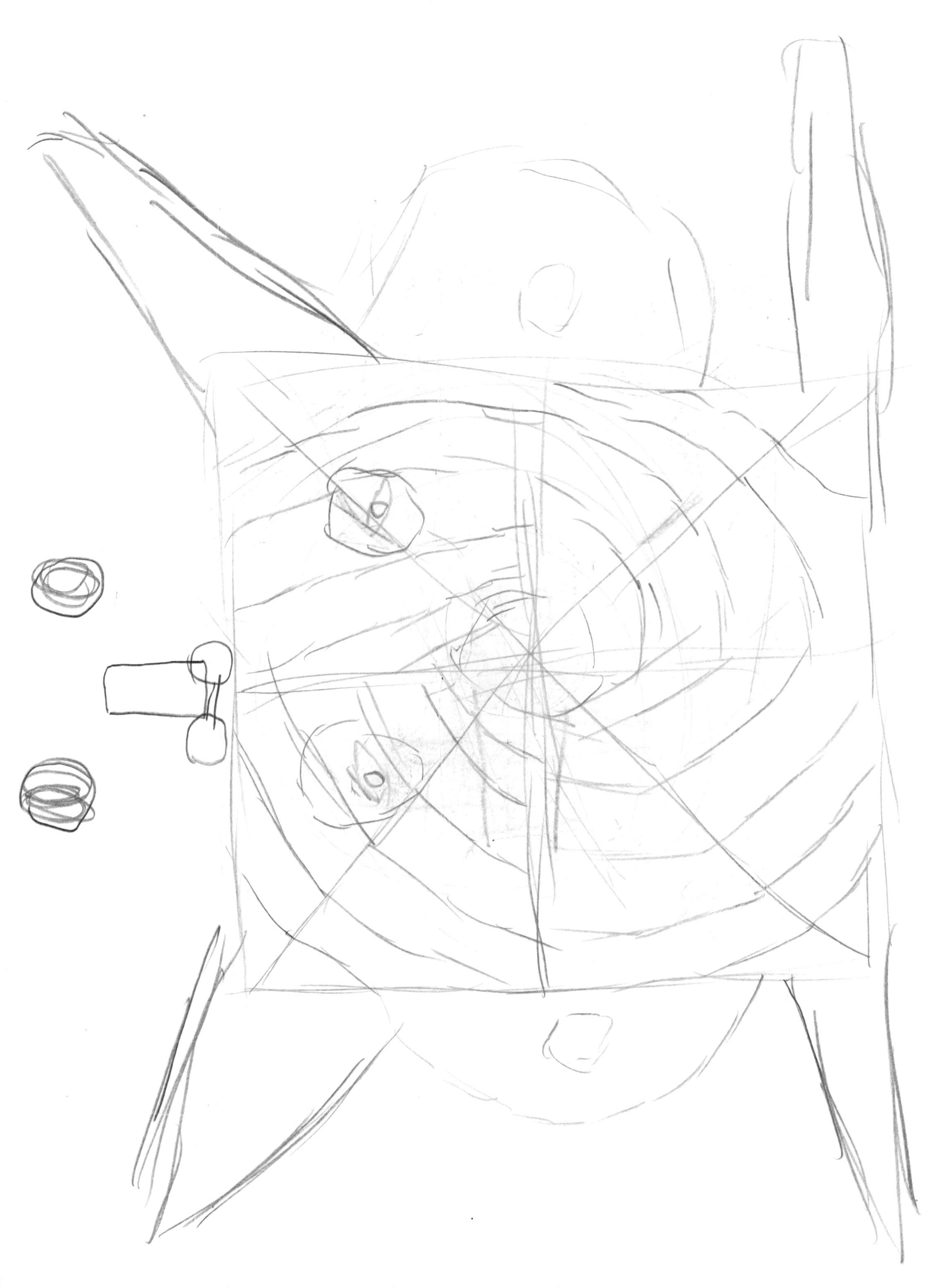

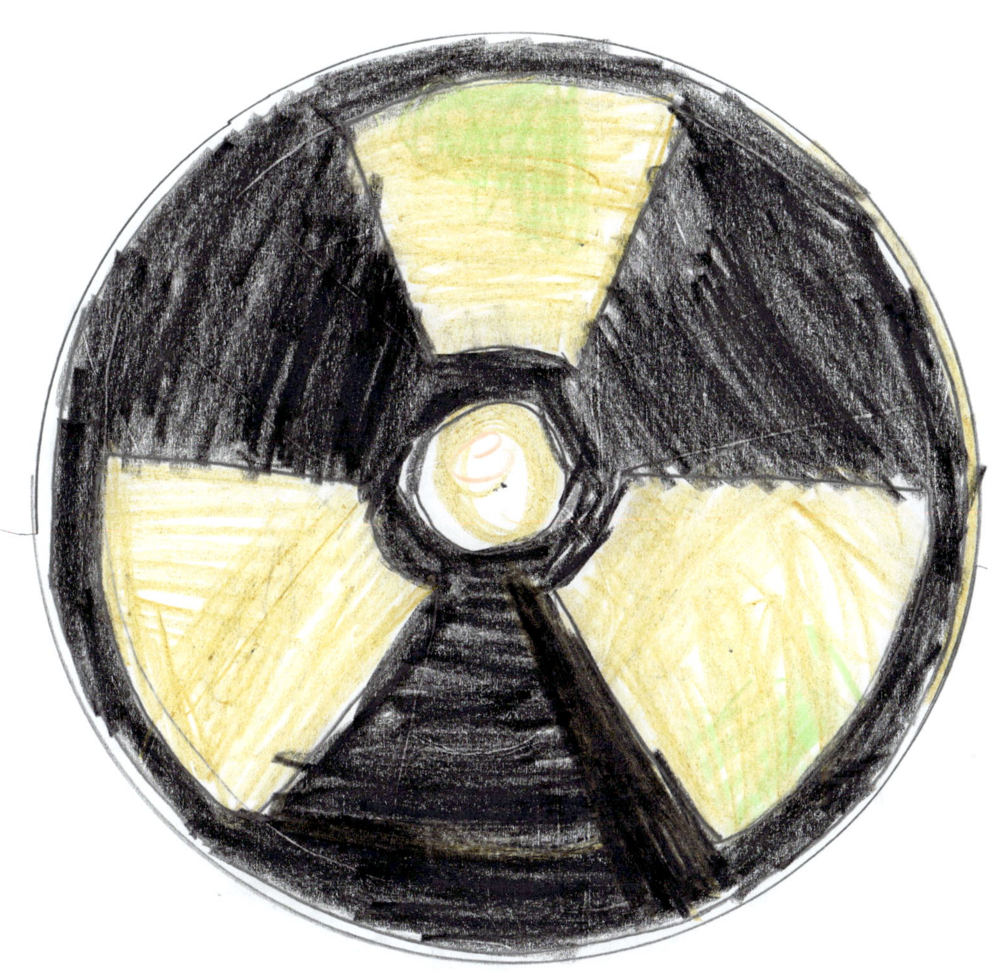

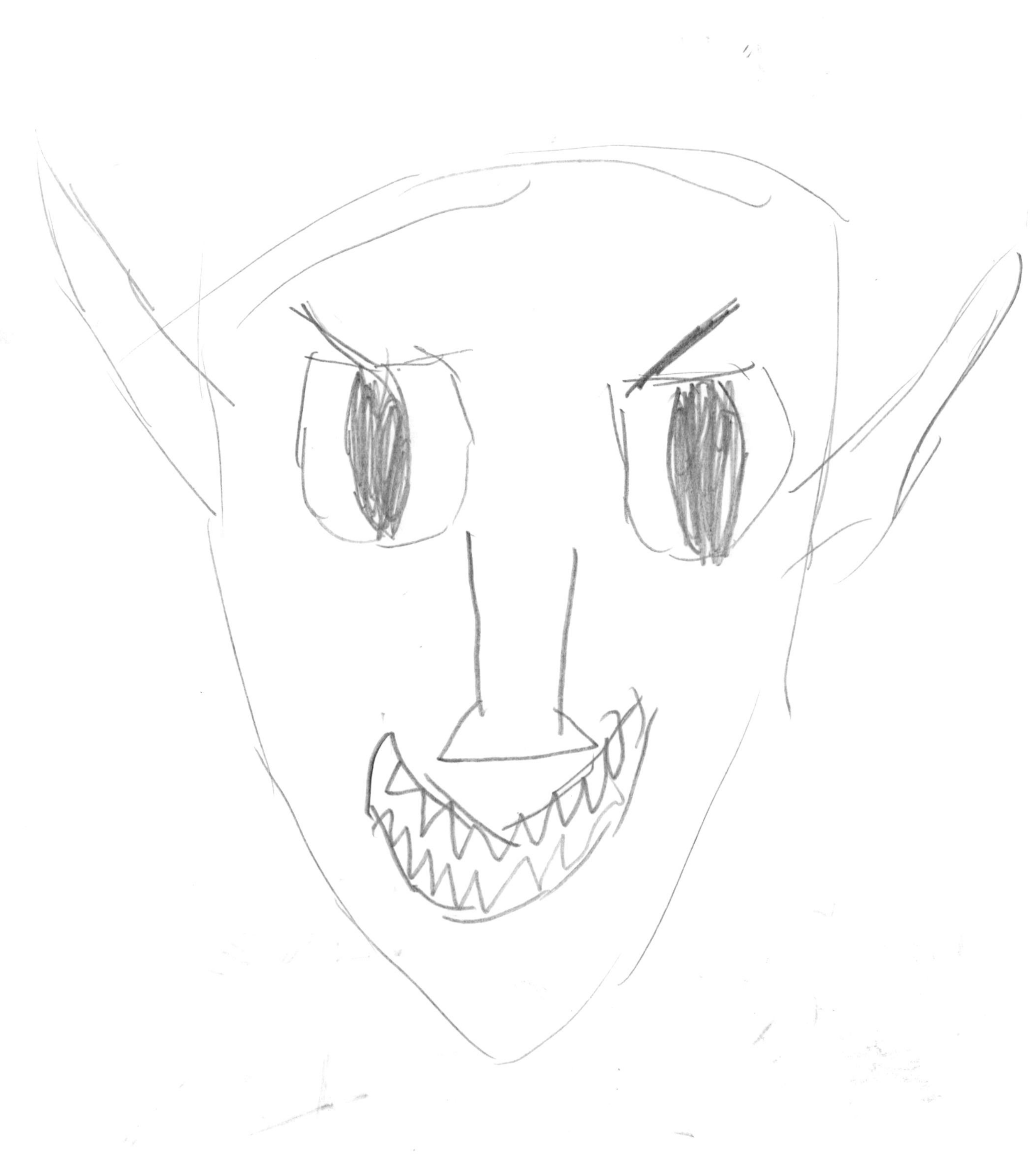

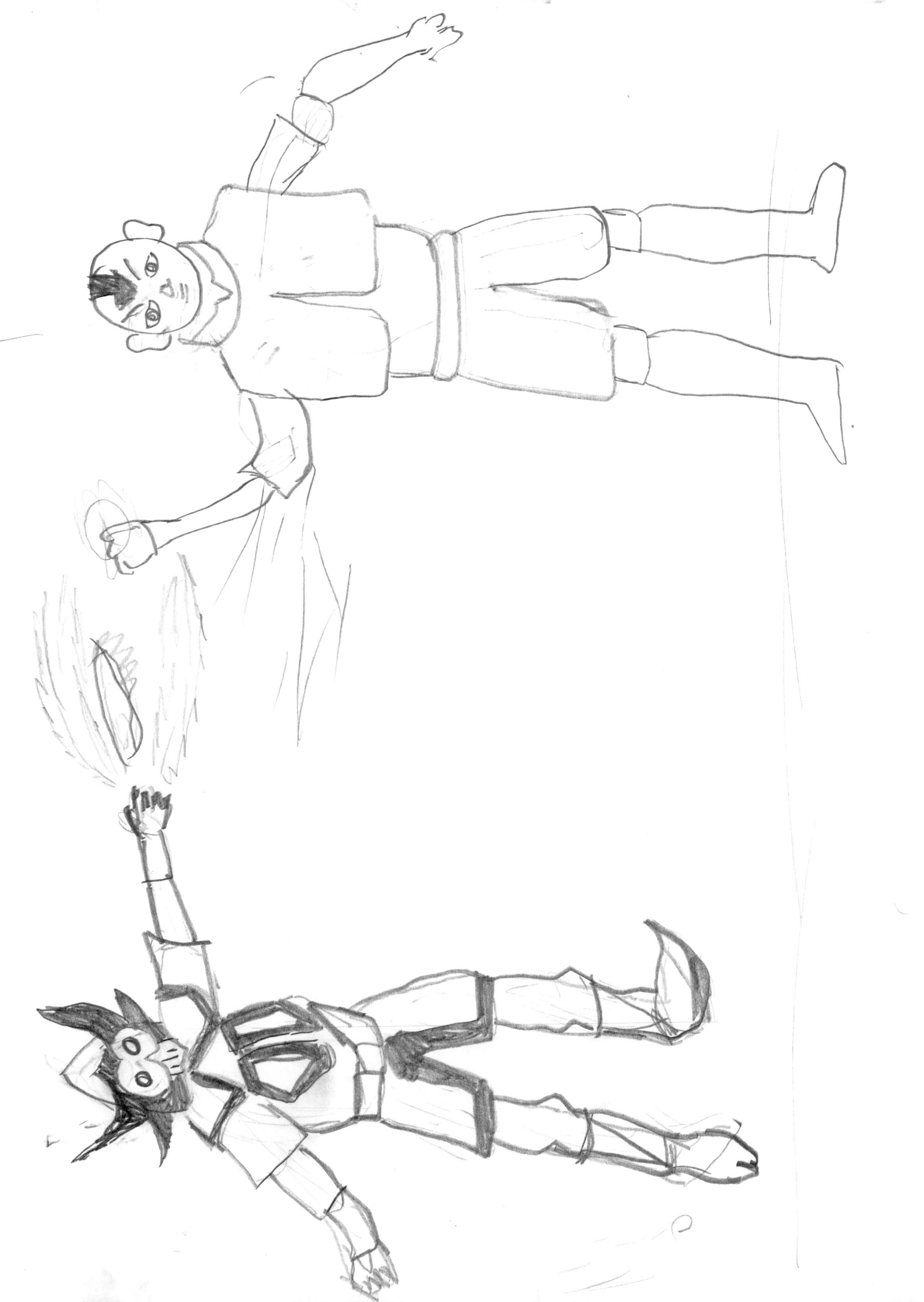

totem pole plan

Dad- thunderbird
mom- bear
sister- fox
me- sun

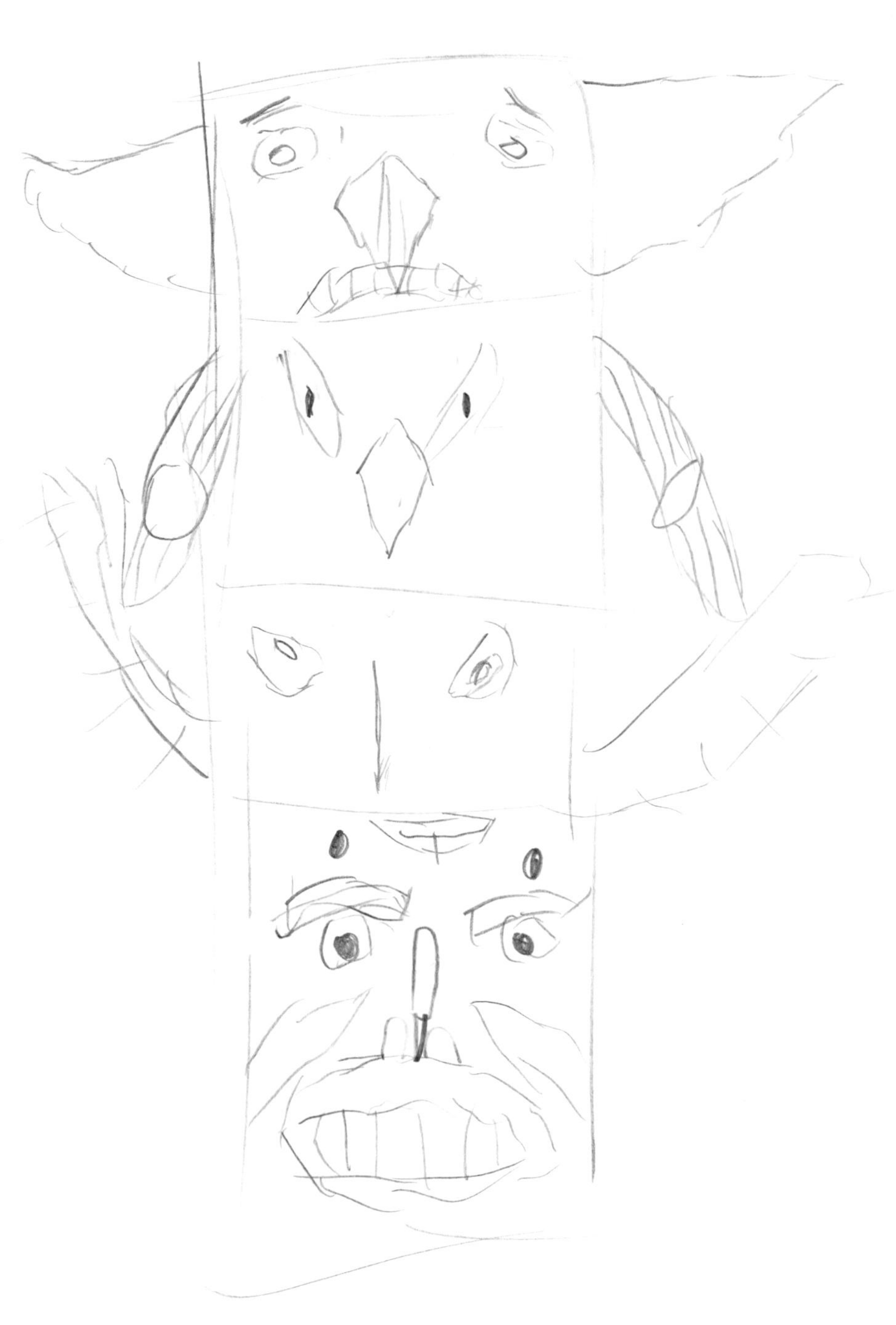

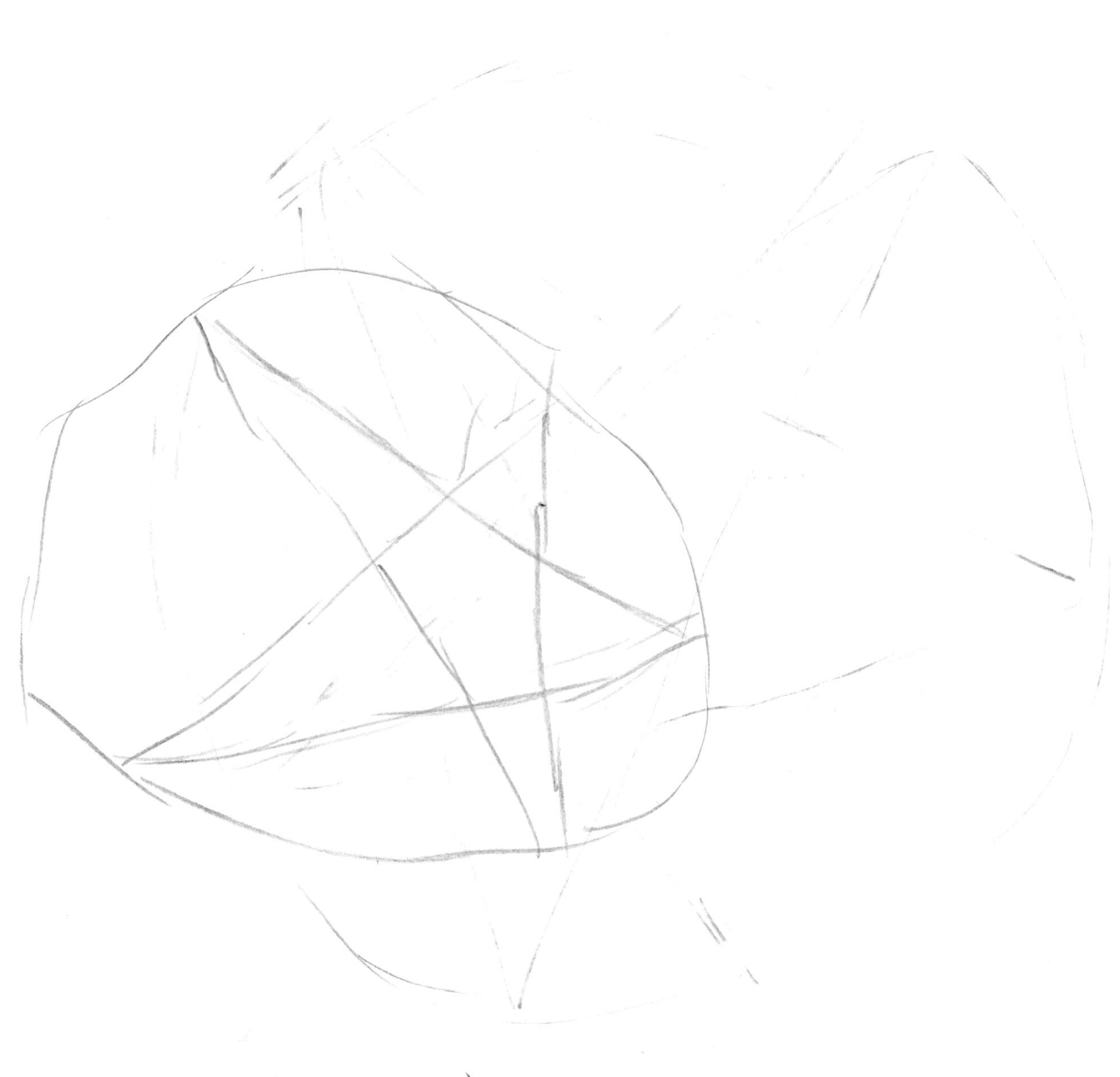

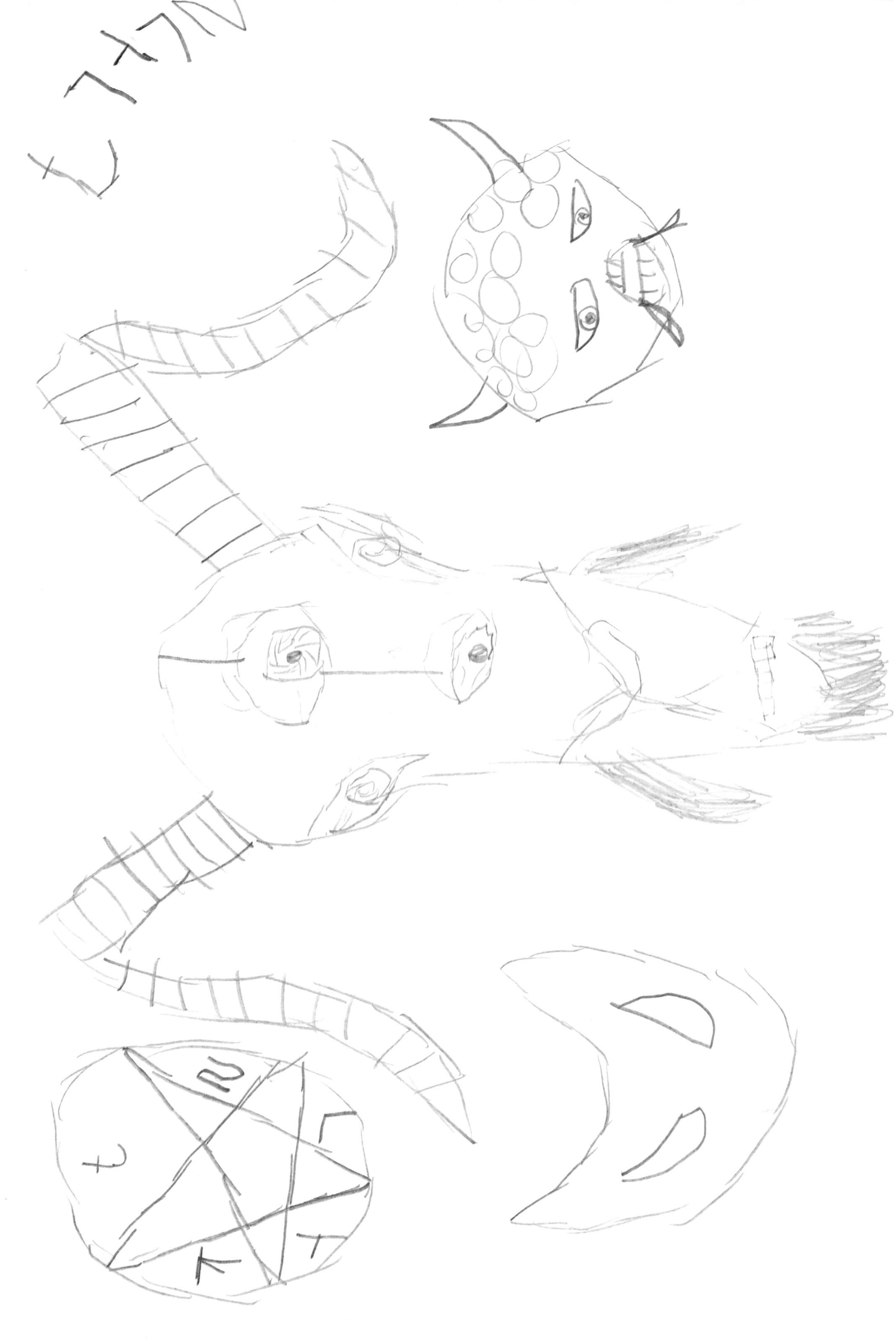

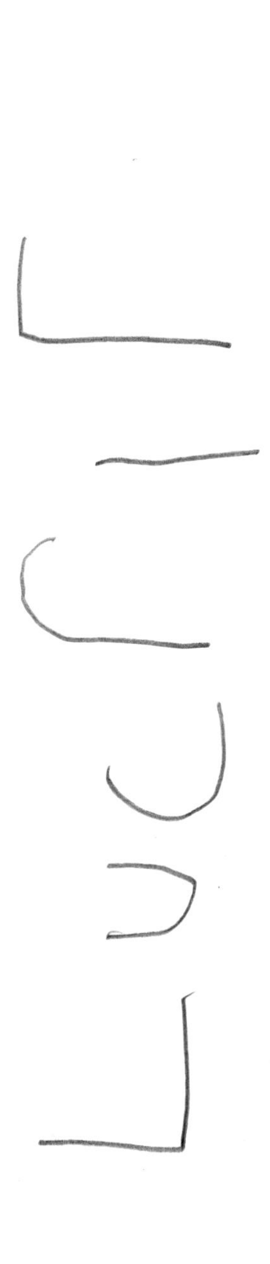

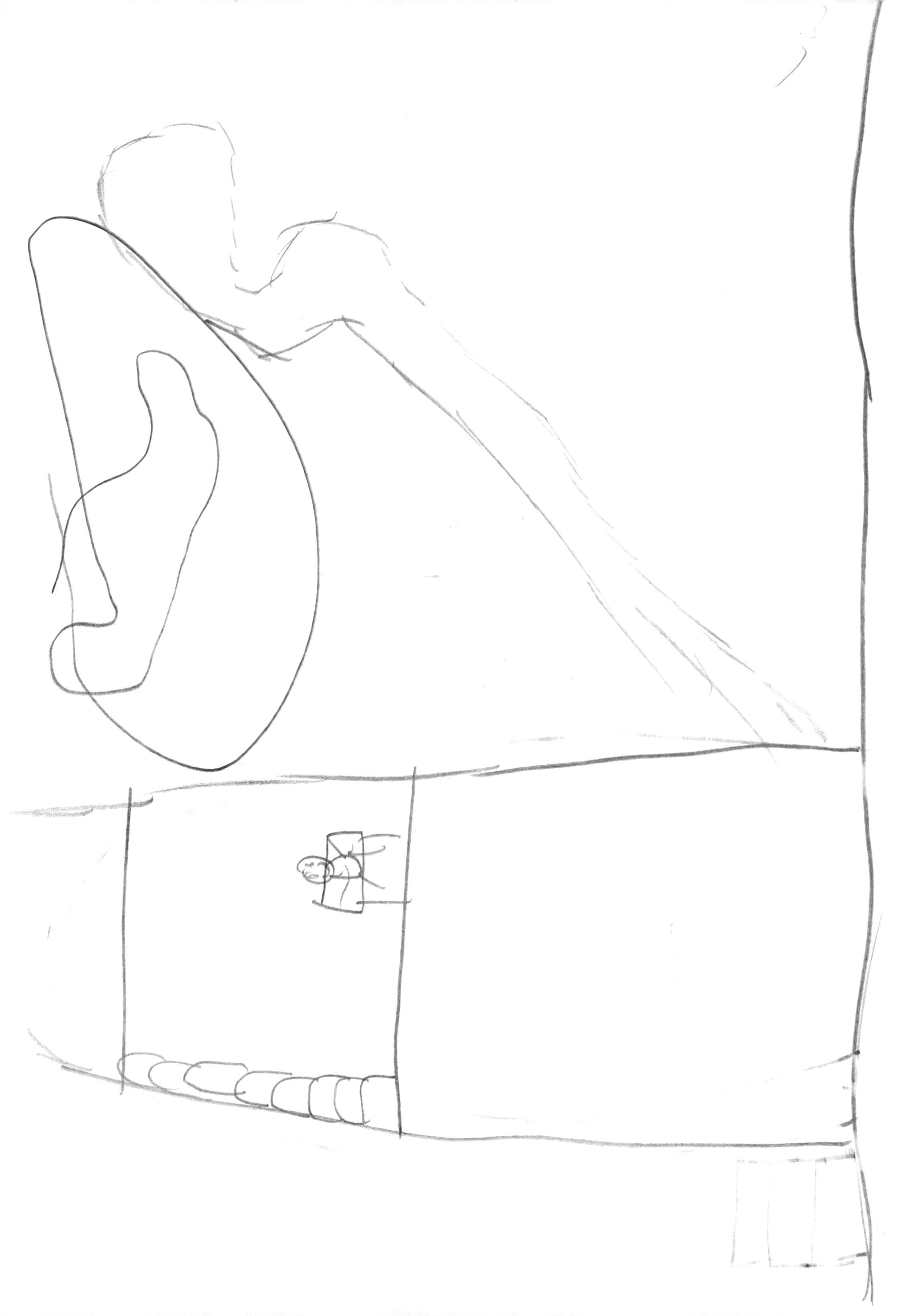

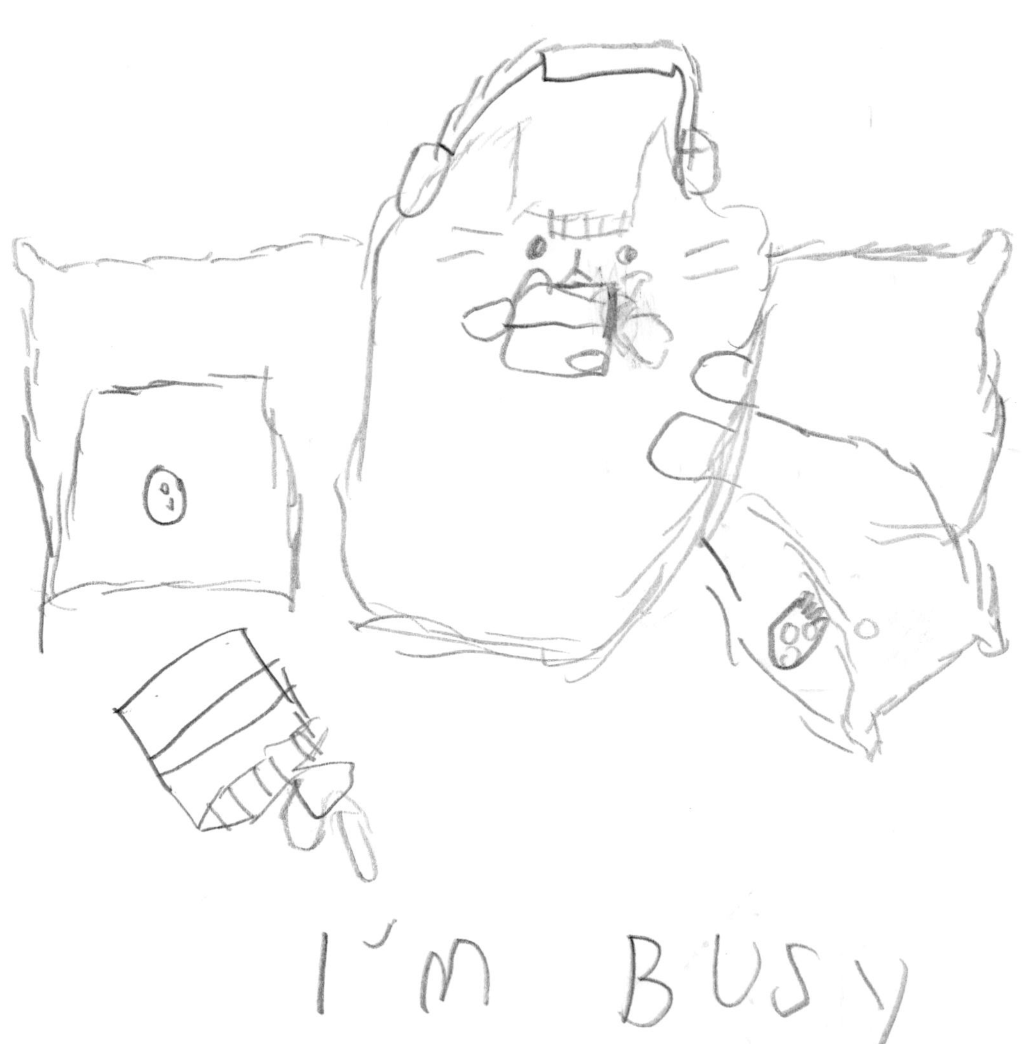
I'M BUSY

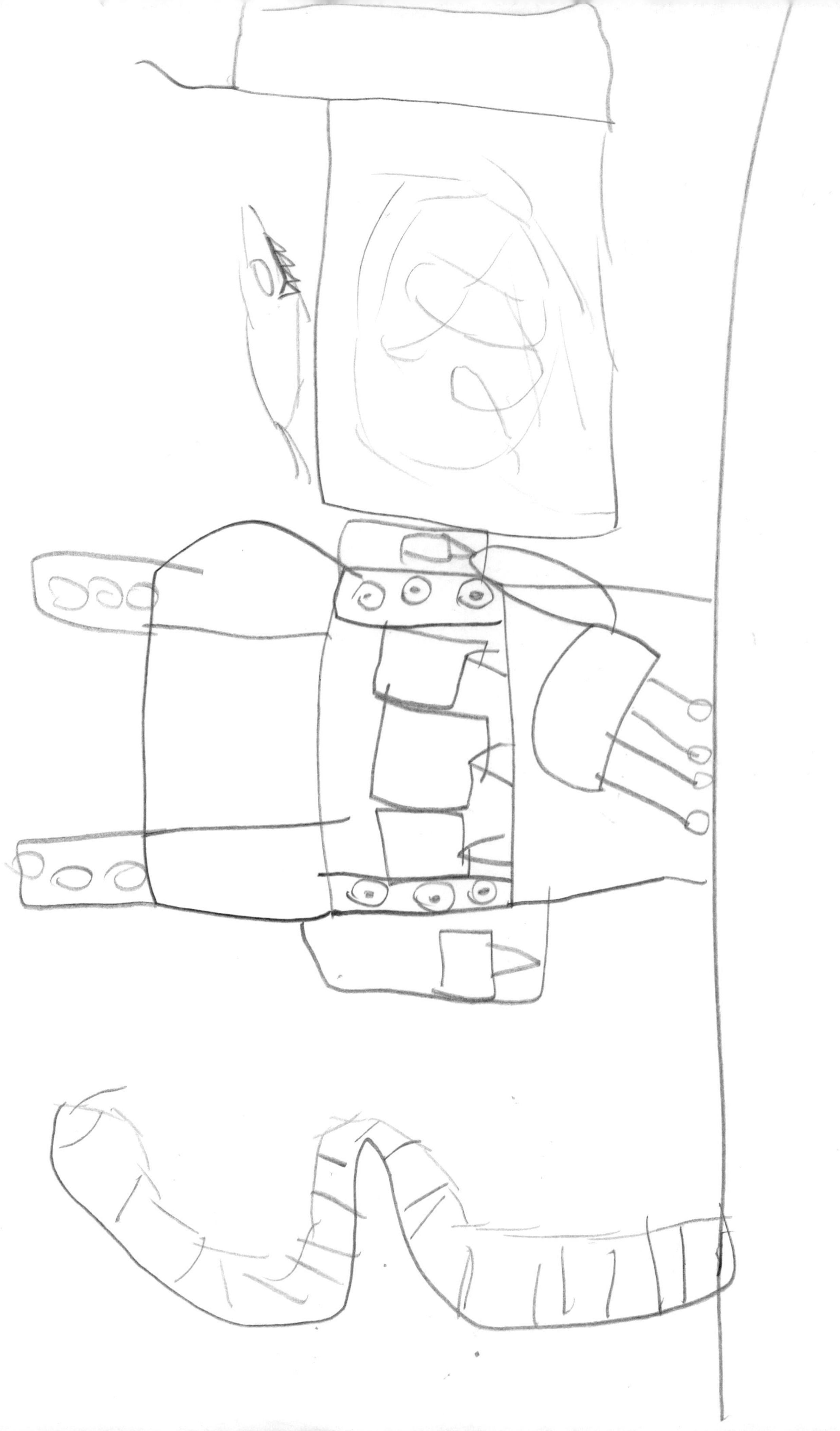

AKUl Sagare

11/2/20

personal and family tradations

controllen

Game

Bike with friends

Bike tire

Animals komodo dragon

dramor art

~~color~~

food pizza

holi

Diwali

wolf ears

the ears turn itno a cup form to listen carefully

bird

inside of ear

chirp

Topic: wolf ears

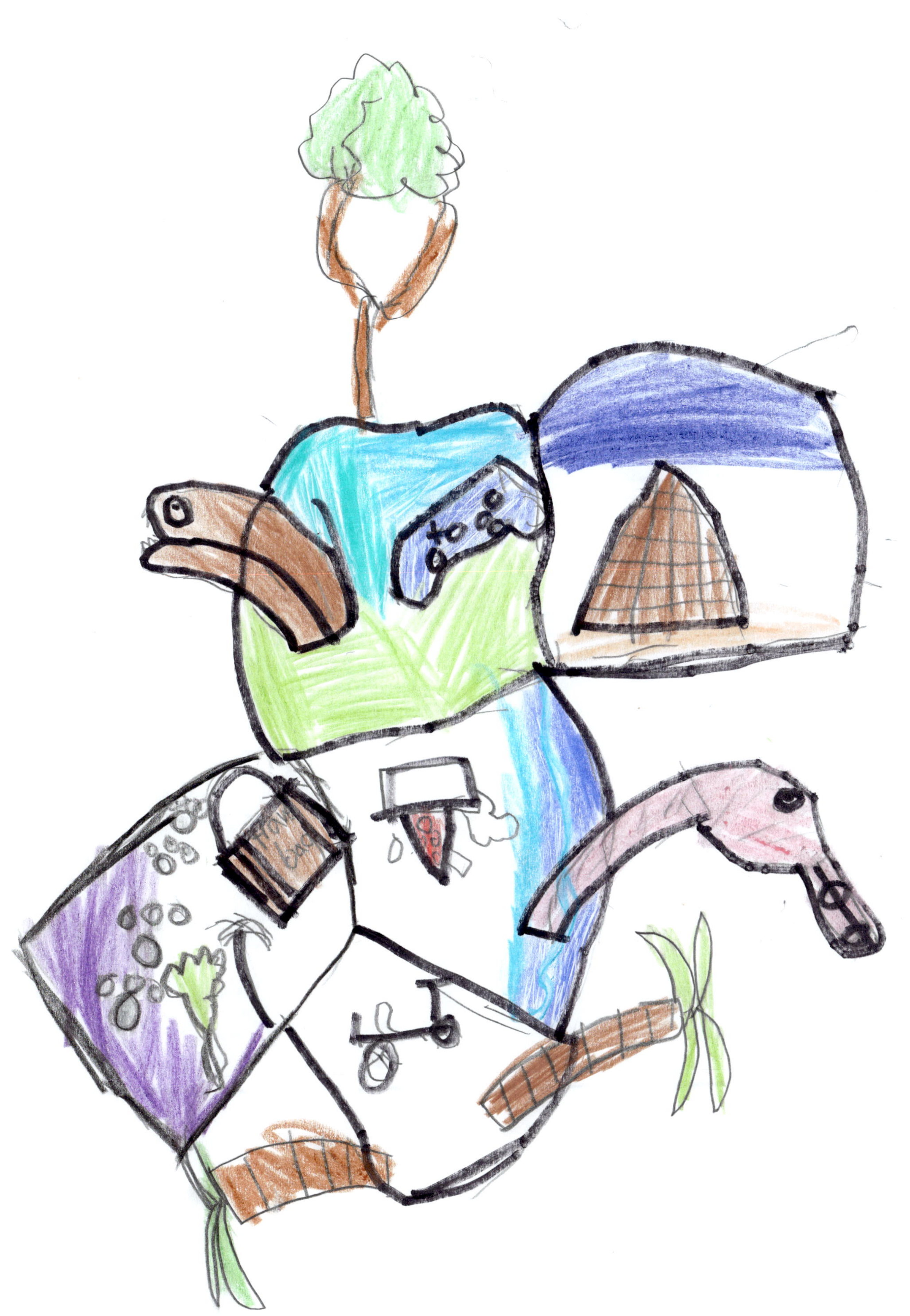

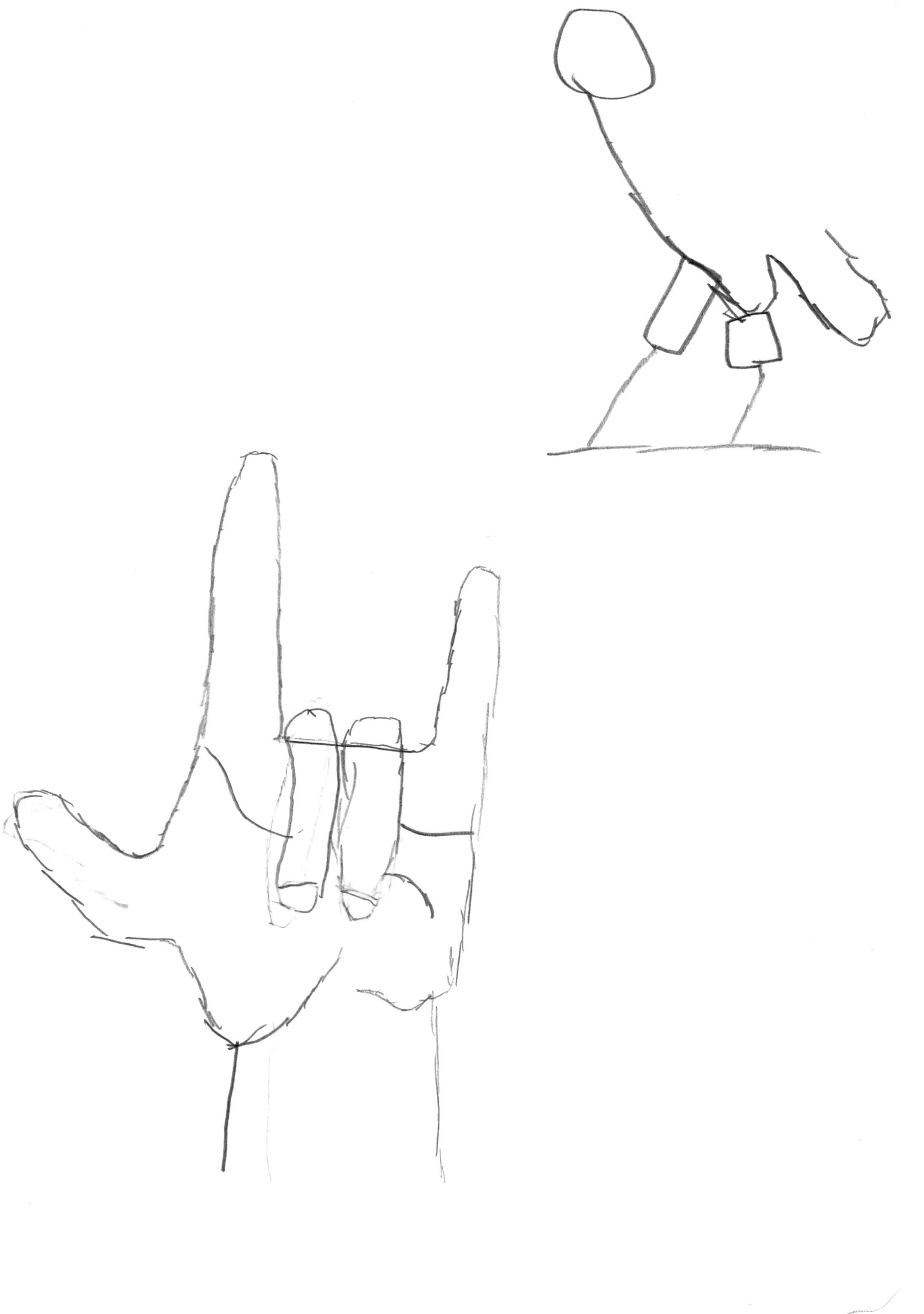

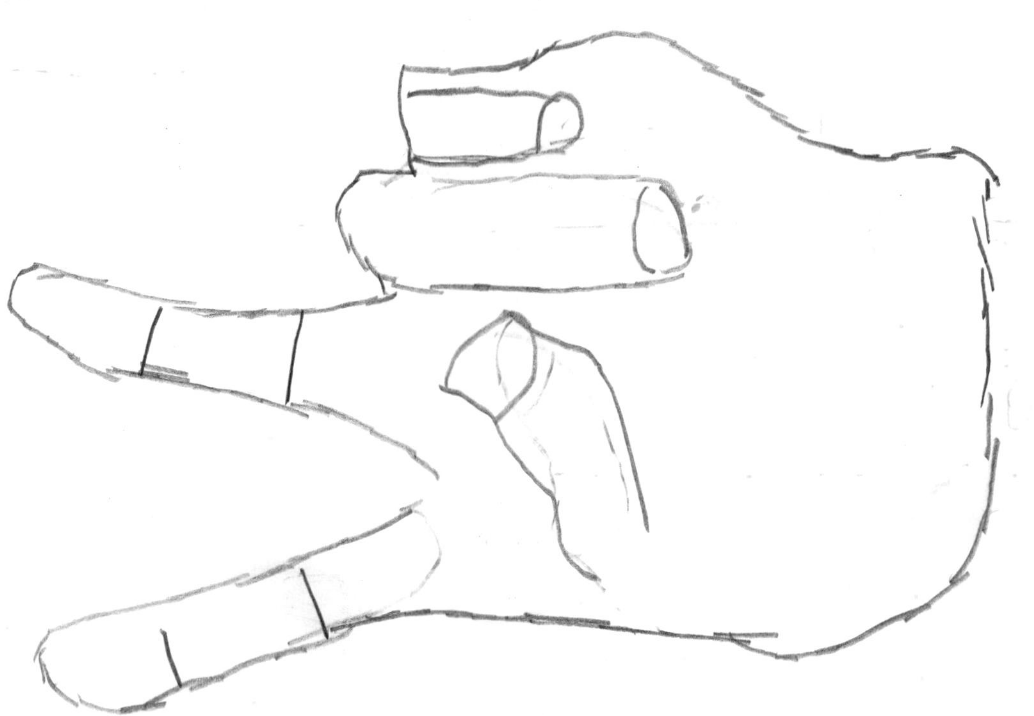

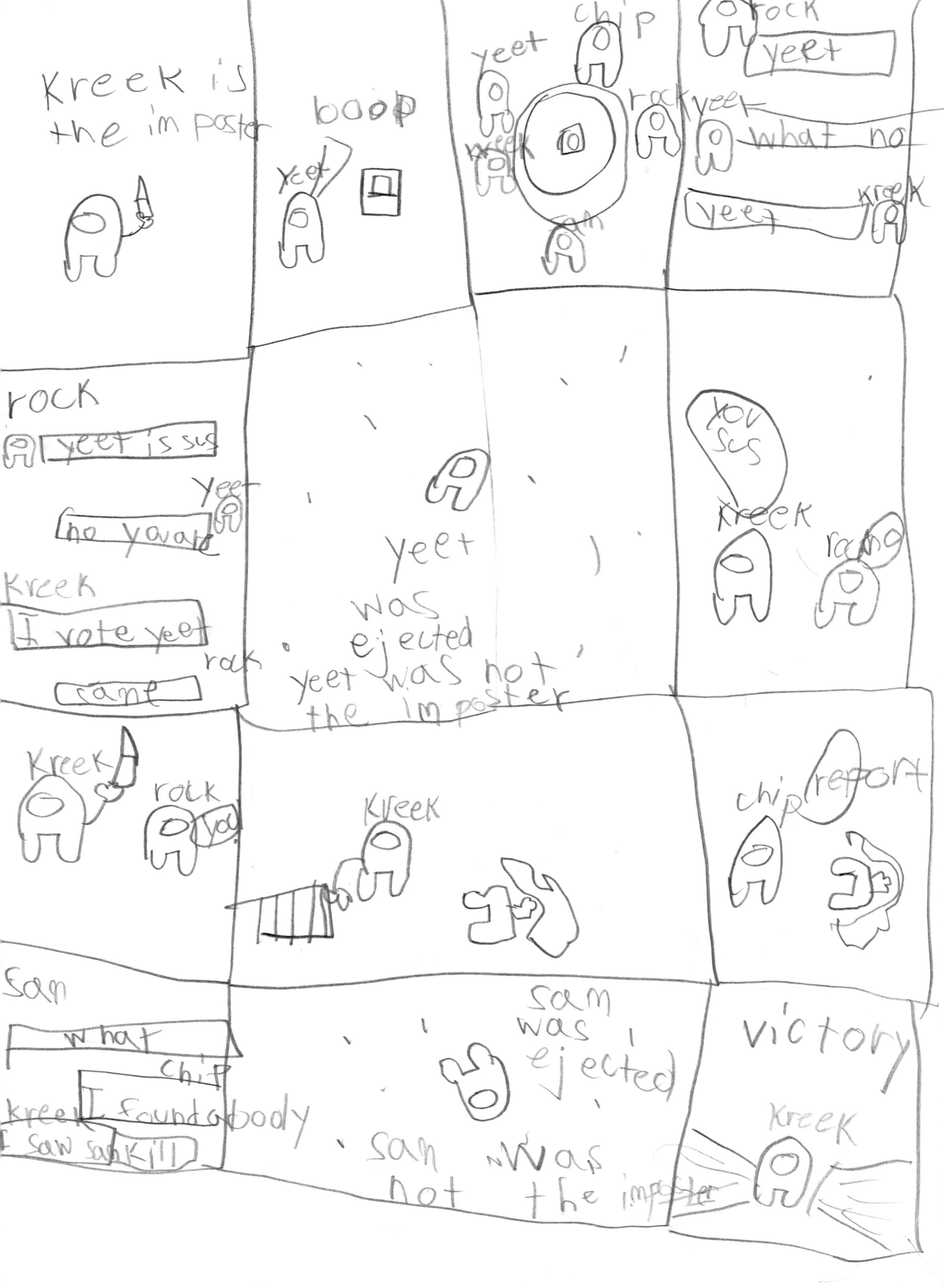
kreek is the imposter
boop
yeet
chip
yeet
rock
kreek
sam
rock
yeet
yeet
what no
kreek
yeet
rock
yeet is sus
yeet
no you are
kreek
I vote yeet
rock
same
yeet was ejected
yeet was not the imposter
you sus
kreek
rock
kreek
rock
you
kreek
chip
report
sam
what
chip
I found a body
kreek
I saw sam kill
sam was ejected
sam was not the imposter
victory
kreek

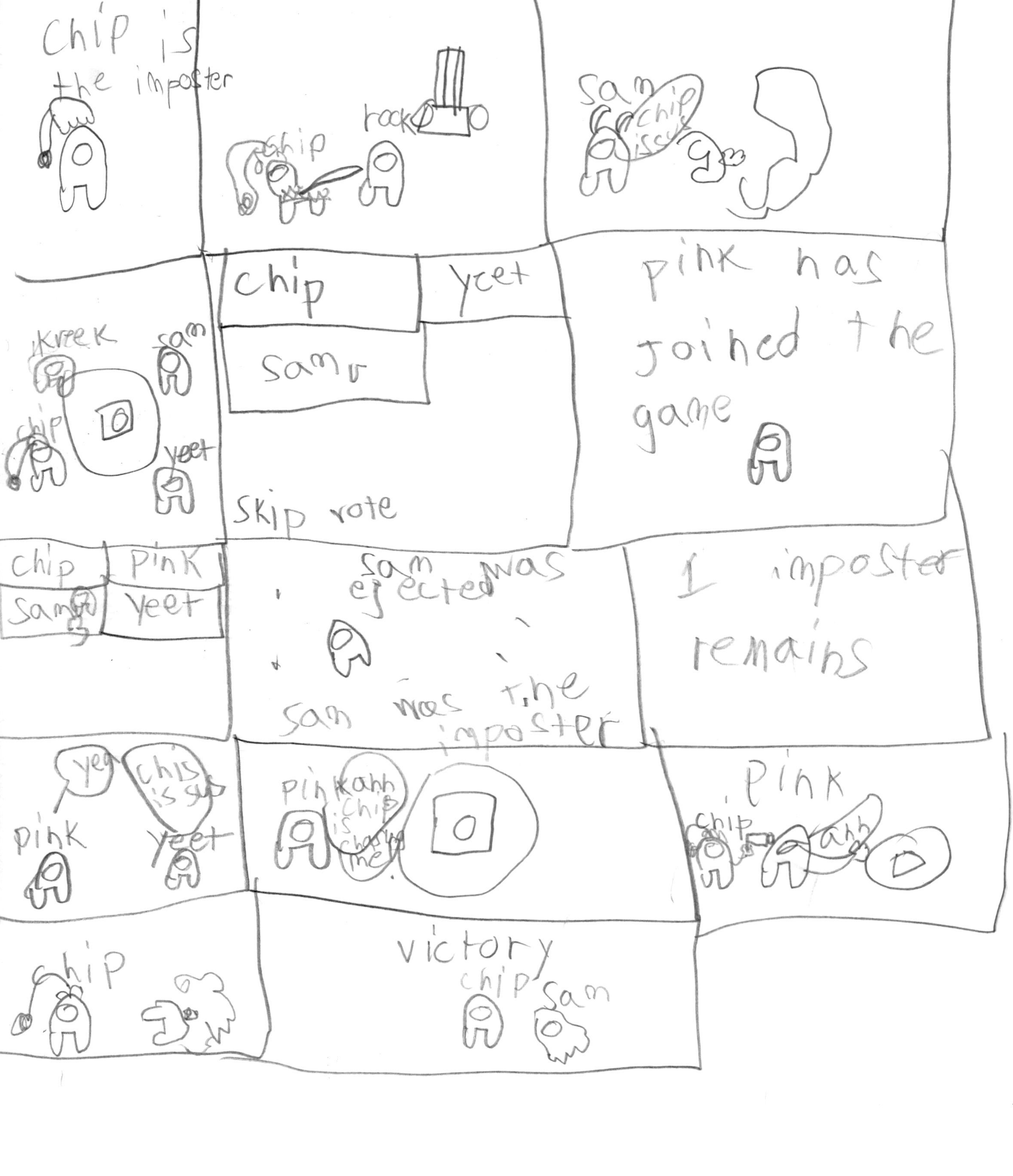

chip is the imposter
chip
rock
sam
chip is sus
kreek
sam
chip
yeet
chip
yeet
sam
skip vote
pink has joined the game
chip
pink
sam
yeet
sam was ejected
sam was the imposter
1 imposter remains
yea
chis is sus
pink
yeet
pink
ahh chip is chasing me
pink
chip
ahh
chip
victory
chip
sam

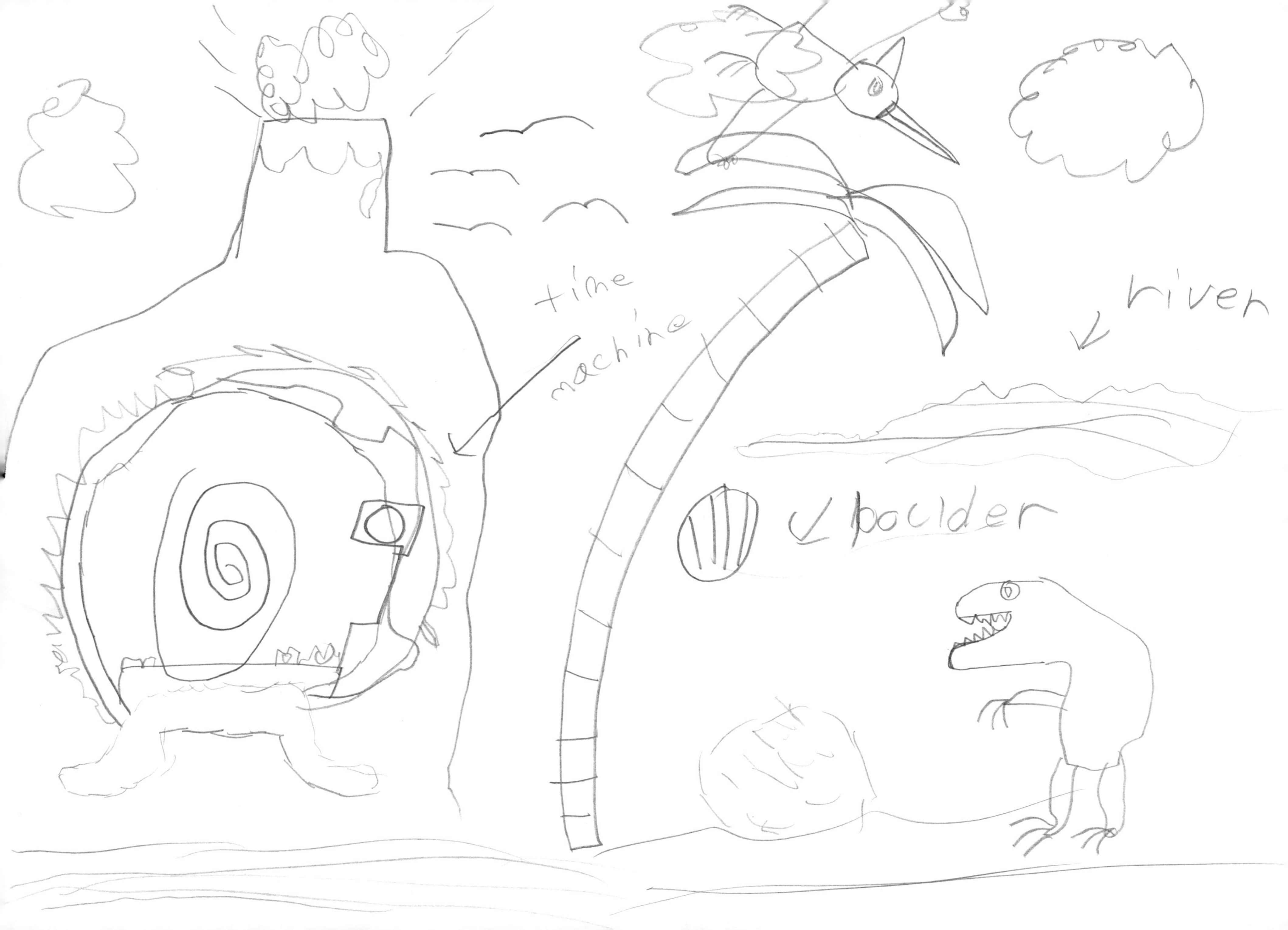
time
machine
river
boulder

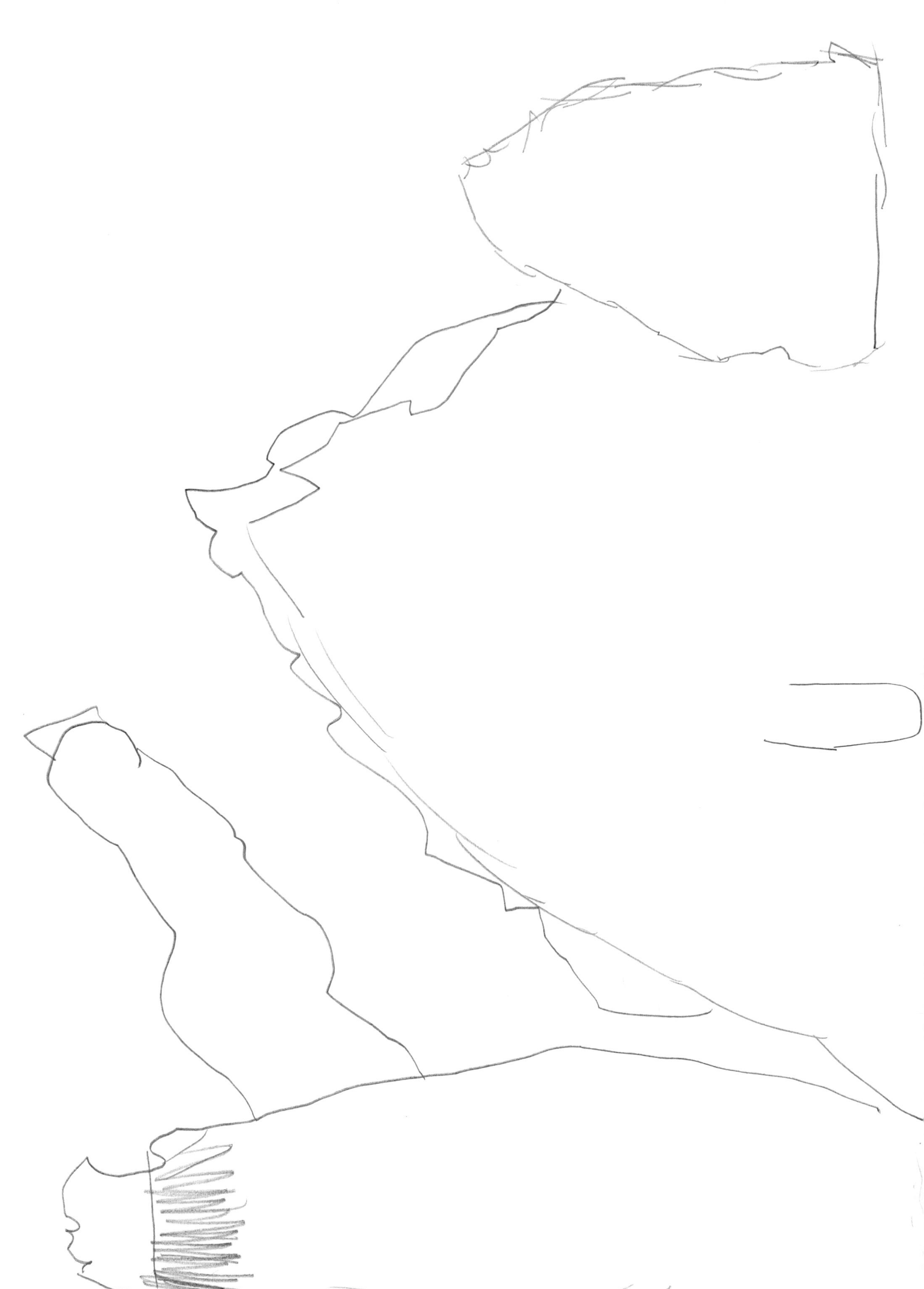

/

akul sagare589@gmail .com

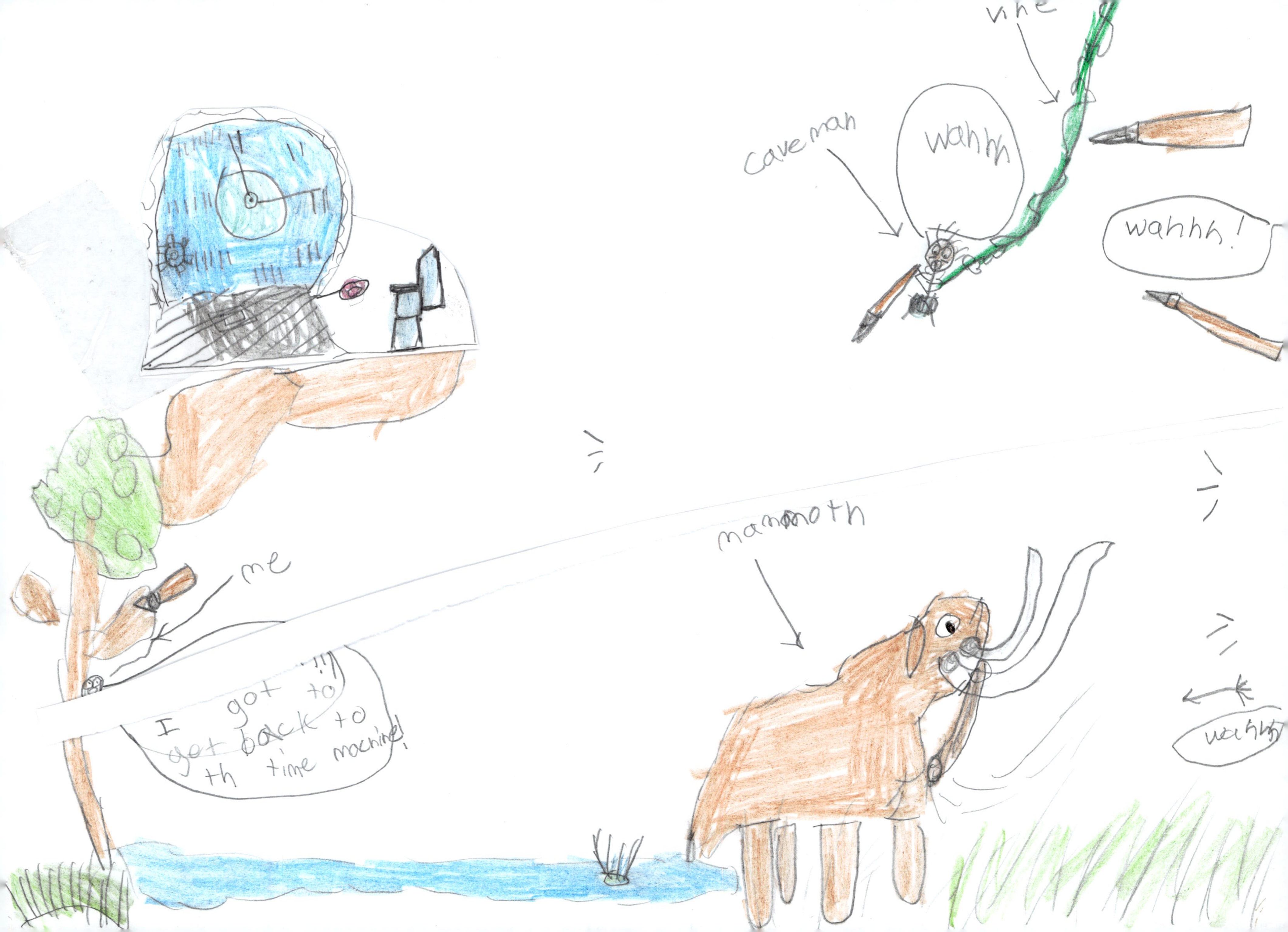
vine
caveman
wahhh
wahhh!
mammoth
me
I got to get back to th time machine!

Twitch

us — Gozterp 30000

pas — Atoz12368dvhg

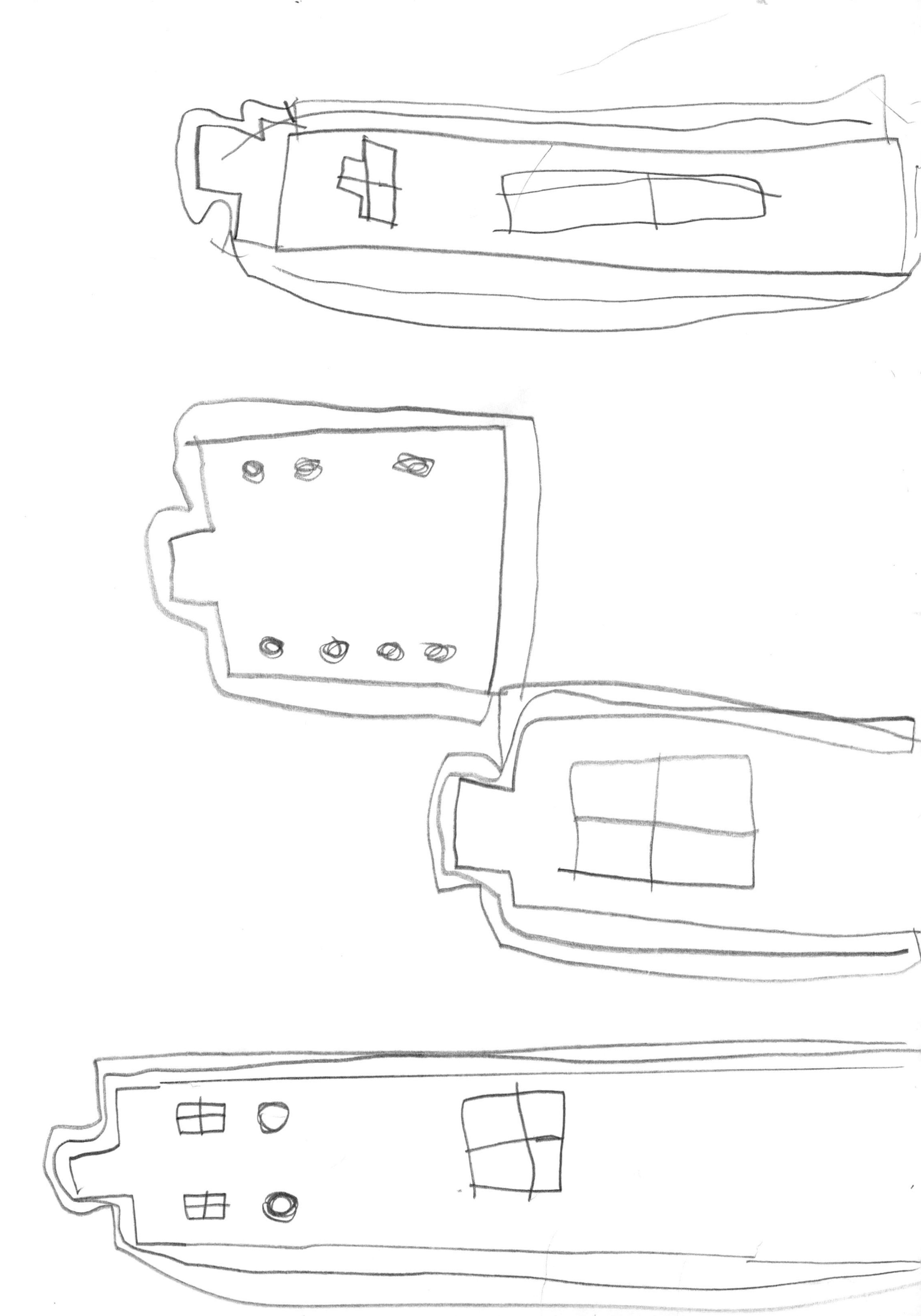

Deal with it 50r

Beast mask 30r

Secret kid wizard 90r

mon opolist mustache 20r

Comedey 31r

30
+20
31
81

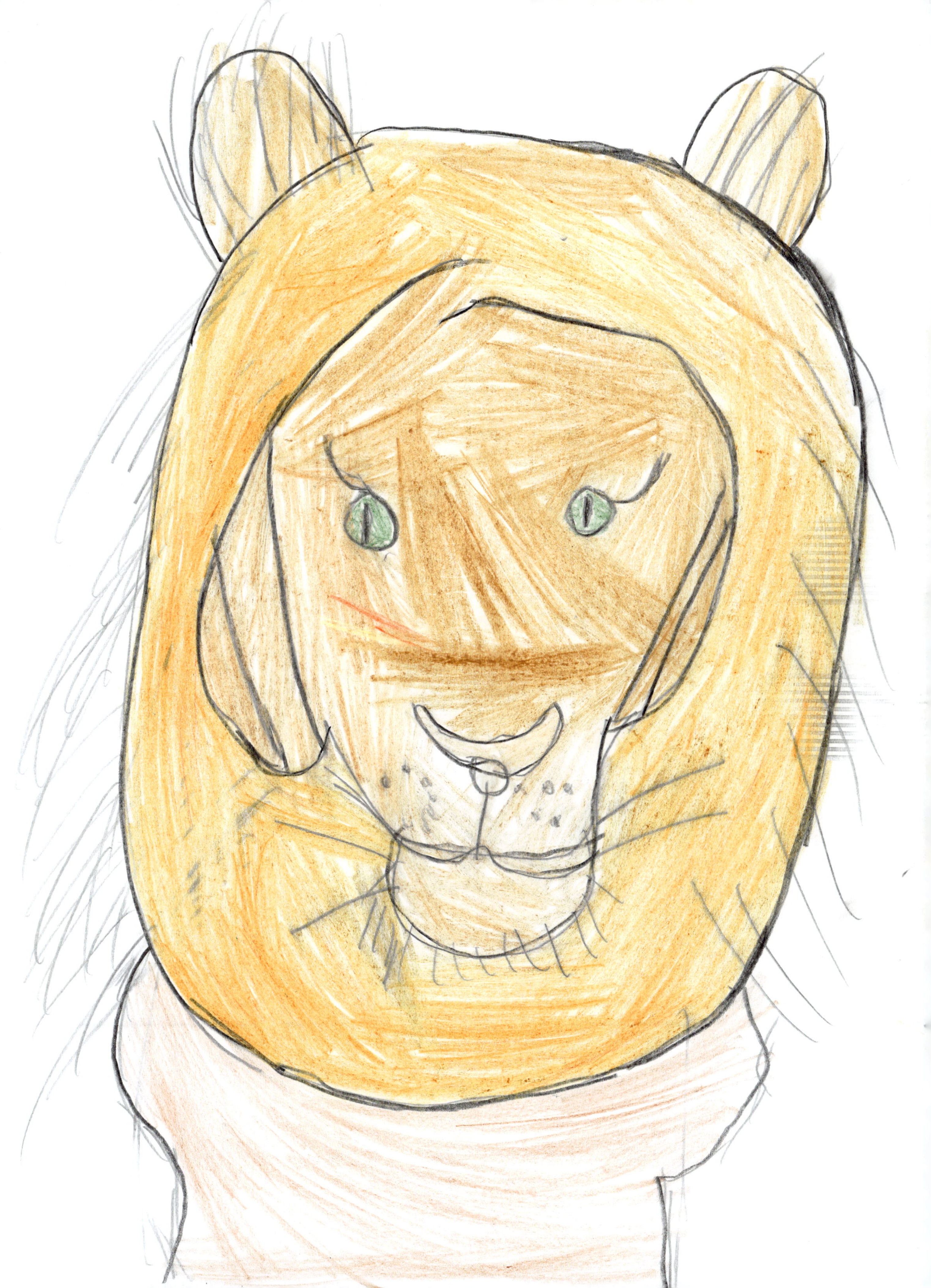

ゴミ箱

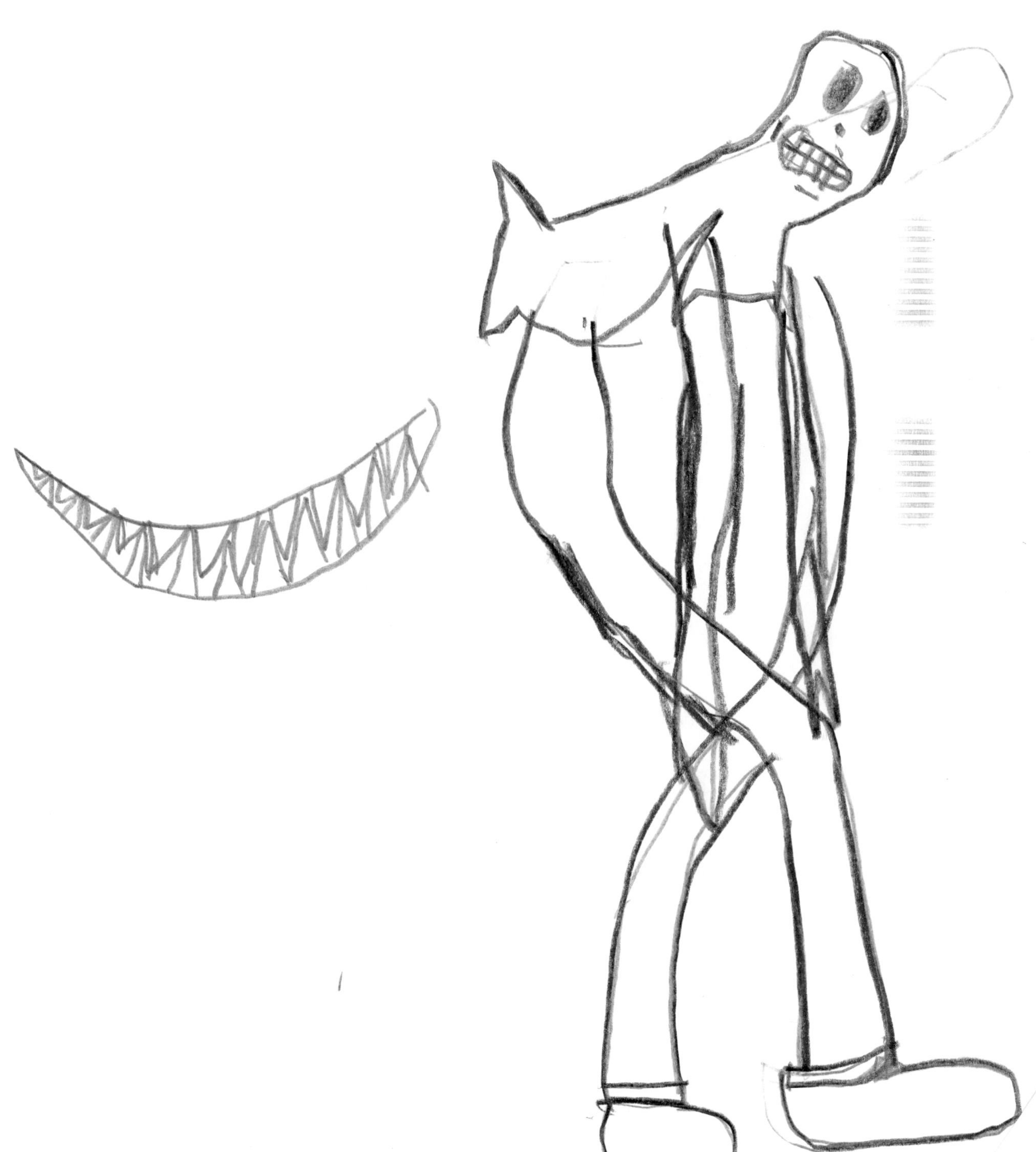

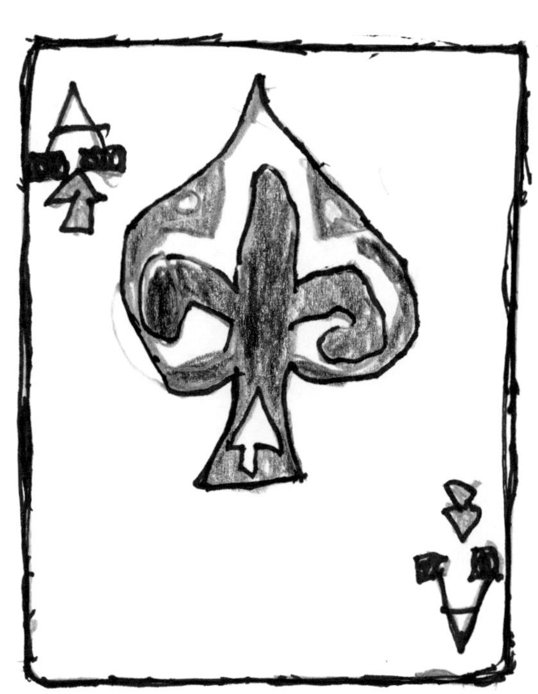

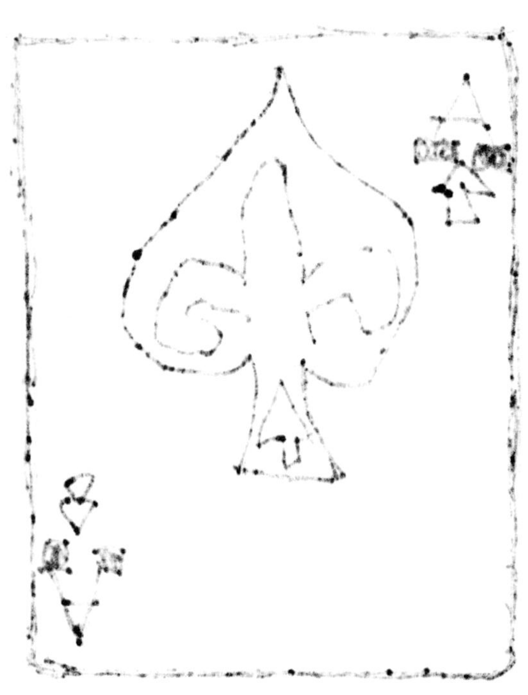

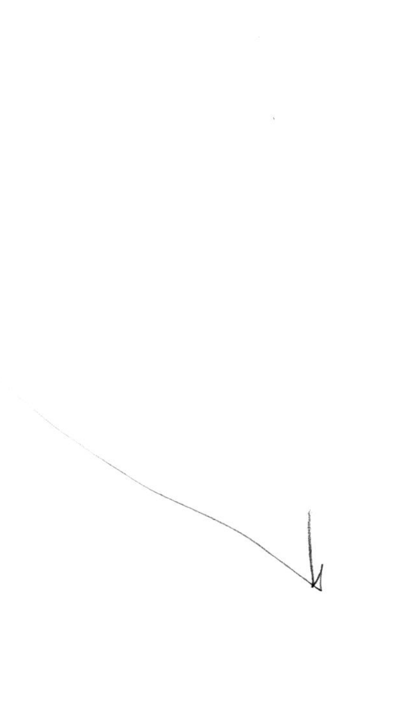